APPROVED MARKETING PLANS

for New Products and Services

APPROVED MARKETING PLANS

for New Products and Services

Dr. Ken K. Wong

U21Global | University of Toronto

iUniverse, Inc.
New York Bloomington

Approved Marketing Plans for New Products and Services

iUniverse books may be ordered through booksellers or by contacting:

iUniverse
1663 Liberty Drive
Bloomington, IN 47403
www.iuniverse.com
1-800-Authors (1-800-288-4677)

Because of the dynamic nature of the Internet, any Web addresses or links contained in this book may have changed since publication and may no longer be valid. The views expressed in this work are solely those of the author and do not necessarily reflect the views of the publisher, and the publisher hereby disclaims any responsibility for them.

ISBN: 978-1-4502-6248-4 (sc)
ISBN: 978-1-4502-6249-1 (ebook)

Printed in the United States of America

iUniverse rev. date: 10/22/2010

To my wife Winnie, and my family members Hello Ma, Hello Dad and Hello Chiu

Thank you for your love, understanding, patience, and confidence.

About the Author

Dr. Ken Kwong-Kay Wong

Dr. Ken K. Wong is a U21Global Marketing Professor and Subject Area Coordinator, training corporate executives and MBA students from over 70 countries. In 2008 and 2009, he received the Faculty Excellence Award, and was honoured in all three award categories, including: Outstanding Professor, Most Innovative Professor and Excellence in Online Education. Since 2003, Dr. Wong has been developing and lecturing marketing courses at the University of Toronto's School of Continuing Studies and also at various institutions of higher education in North America.

Dr. Wong's research interests include marketing for luxury brands, customer relationship management and online education. His articles have appeared in peer-reviewed international journals such as *Telecommunications Policy, Service Industries Journal,* and *Journal of Database Marketing and Customer Strategy Management.* Dr. Wong is also the author of the SCS lecture series in the areas of International Marketing, Advertising, PR & Publicity, E-Business, and Retail Merchandising. His latest work includes *Avoiding Plagiarism: Write Better Papers in APA, Chicago and Harvard Citation Styles, Discovering Marketing in 38 Hours* and *CRM in Action: Maximizing Value Through Market Segmentation, Product Differentiation & Customer Retention.*

Prior to entering the academic field, Dr. Wong was the Vice President of Marketing at

TeraGo Networks (TSX: TGO) and had previously served as Director of eProduct Marketing at the e-commerce division of PSINet (NASDAQ: PSIX). He had also carried progressive product marketing roles at Sprint Canada and TELUS Mobility.

Certified by the American Marketing Association as a Professional Certified Marketer, Dr. Wong completed his Bachelor of Science degree at the University of Toronto and holds the International MBA degree from Nyenrode Business Universiteit in the Netherlands. He earned his Doctor of Business Administration degree from the University of Newcastle, Australia and has completed executive education programmes at both Kellogg and Queen's.

Table of Contents

Foreword

No branding is better than bad branding. Case in point: Sentosa – Singapore's Island Resort.

The former CEO, Darrell Metzger of Walt Disney fame, is a Californian. He has this uncanny Southern drawl when he talks. On the third day of my job as Marketing Director at Sentosa, Darrell leaned over to me and said "Mauriceeee, whadoyou make of those alphabets 'S L G' painted on those darn dustbinnnns..!" And I, the new bright-eyed and bushy-tailed Head of Marketing, proudly proclaimed, "I think it stands for Sentosa Leisure Group, Darrell." The CEO then replied, "Is that what you call Marketing? Do we really need to brand dustbins? Is that why we have you!?"

The new Marketing Director's first task was to paint over the 800 plus dustbins scattered over the 390-hectare island of Sentosa. Marketing you see, has to be just a tad ahead of the existing environment. Marketing must always be relevant to the constantly shifting landscape, whilst at the same time, it has to be consistent. If a vision and mission has been determined, stick to it. Make it work, make it relevant, and find a way to make it look good! Consistent concentration. This not only refers to look and style but also where and which channels were chosen for which to work through. Marketing does require some eyeballs, however it is far more important to focus on whose eyeballs it left 'what' impression on.

I have had the pleasure of knowing Ken Wong this last decade but in that time as my lecturer, mentor and friend. Ken continues to significantly influence my continued work in the realms of Marketing Management and E-Marketing specifically. His latest work exemplifies the unassuming and straightforward style he is so famous for. Ken has obviously worked very hard to make things easy for the reader. The work is a step-by-step, logical, detailed and multi-faceted approach to writing the all-important Marketing plan.

This latest work represents a resource that can be counted upon to clearly draw distinction between the confusing, overlapping backdrop of business and marketing plans. And just when you thought the all too familiar topic of Marketing could not be represented in an even more simplified manner; Ken has once again raised the bar. The usefulness of this book is also in its revelation of how the links between the Marketing function and the other faculty's of Human Resource, Finance, Operations and so on take place. There also is rigor built in this serial manner.

Finally I would like to point out that Professor Wong has chosen to incorporate working examples alongside proven, tried and tested marketing principles that formulate the basis for good and solid presentations and further discussion for the developed plan. As to how exactly the 'Repainting of Dustbins' was a consequence of Sentosa's Marketing Plan. Well I guess you will have to read the book to find that out.

Maurice Williams, PMC

Maurice Williams has over 20 years of experience in marketing and sales management, carrying roles such as CMO of SingPost and Marketing Director of Sentosa. He is a member of Economic Branding Task Force and Ministry of Trade & Industry's Integrated Resort Selection Committee. Maurice is a Certified Practising Management Consultant, he has lectured at Nanyang Polytechnic's School of Business Management and other institutions of higher education in Singapore.

Preface

You've got lots of great ideas to grow your organization's business and you've presented them to the management team. The VPs seem to be nodding their heads and you feel great...until they say, "That's excellent, send us a detailed marketing plan by Monday morning, alright? Next."

"A marketing plan? I thought you listened to my Powerpoint presentation!?" you wonder.

The unfortunate reality in the business world is that talk is cheap. Whether you are working in a large multi-national corporation or a small local firm, great ideas have to be presented in a marketing plan for management review. Otherwise, things won't happen even if your suggestions are brilliant.

So what possessed me to spend time writing such a book? Despite the fact that there are already tons of great marketing textbooks and that it only takes seconds to find writing tips on the Internet, many students are still encountering difficulties in writing their marketing plans. I have graded many marketing plan assignments in the last decade, and I am still shocked to see how students are missing key components in their plans. Unless you have a clear understanding of your marketing needs, those expensive marketing plan software won't help too much because you're required to fill in the blanks in a serial manner. Every week, my e-mail box is filled with student questions like "Dr. Wong, can you tell me how to write a marketing plan? I need to complete one in the next few days."

"Ah, another assignment deadline is coming up!"

While I'm willing to help, you know it's really difficult to explain the details of a marketing plan in an e-mail – which gave me this crazy idea to write a short book on marketing plan development. If you've enjoyed reading my other books such as *Avoiding Plagiarism: Write Better Papers in APA, Chicago and Harvard Citation Styles* and *CRM in Action: Maximizing Value Through Market Segmentation, Product Differentiation & Customer Retention*, I'm sure you will like this piece as well.

Although many of my SCS and MBA students have reviewed the materials presented in this book, I know it's not perfect; in fact, it's far from perfect. As a writer, I'd like to hear your feedback about my little book. Your suggestions will help shape the future edition of this book, so don't feel shy to drop me an e-mail.

Dr. Ken K. Wong

黃廣基 博士

Ottawa, Ontario, Canada
Sep 7, 2010

e-mail: ken.wong@utoronto.ca
e-mail: kwong@u21global.edu.sg
Twitter: http://twitter.com/drkenkwong
Web: http://www.introductiontomarketing.ca

Acknowledgement

In completing my book, I have drawn support from many people and thus feel a huge debt of gratitude. I would like to thank the International Editorial Board for providing me with valuable input and constructive criticism to my work. The preparation of the marketing plan examples would not have been possible without the help of my MBA students and their assistance is appreciated.

International Editorial Board:

Abdalla Gholoum
Annie Nyet Ngo Chan
Basil Pathrose
Chee Wai Hoo
Dutta Bholanath
Ekaterina Leonova
Engelbert Atangana
LH Kho
Khurshid Jussawalla
Kishore Pai
Lothar R. Pehl
Narendra Nesarikar
Rajen Kumar Shah
Richard Anthony
Shama Dewji
Tasneem Tailor
Vicky Yan Xu
Vien Cortes
Zulfikar Jiffry

MBA Students:

Scott Ratté
Vineet Sinha
Jason Mack
Sue Mercer
Christopher Erlandsen
Ashley Gerry
Jessica Malcolmson
Darya Bushmakin
Edward Walsh
Mike Prieskorn
Galen Burleigh

Chapter 1 – Introduction

Marketing Plan vs. Business Plan

There are many reasons you would need to write a marketing plan. Perhaps you're trying to raise some money from venture capitalists for your start-up operation and need to spin a beautiful picture about your business, or you're trying to get the bank to lend you more money for your business expansion. Some need to write a marketing plan on a quarterly or annual basis as part of their regular job duties. If my guess is correct, quite a bit of you are reading this book because your marketing plan homework assignment is due in a week's time and you have no idea where to start the writing process. Alright, I'm going to show you how to write one. First, however, you need to ask yourself this question:

"Am I writing a marketing plan or a business plan?"

The answer really depends on your situation, industry, and context. In general, a full-blown business plan discusses not only marketing, but also areas like distribution, IT/operations, finance, and human resources in roughly equal weight.

If you are running a small operation, say, a three-person bakeshop, then your business plan will look similar to a marketing plan, as I doubt you will spend too much time talking about your IIR and finance concerns. However, if you are working in a large organization, the marketing plan you are writing will probably be later consolidated into a "corporate plan" together with other plans as submitted by the managers in other functional areas.

The following diagram gives you a visual presentation on where the marketing plan fits into the overall picture:

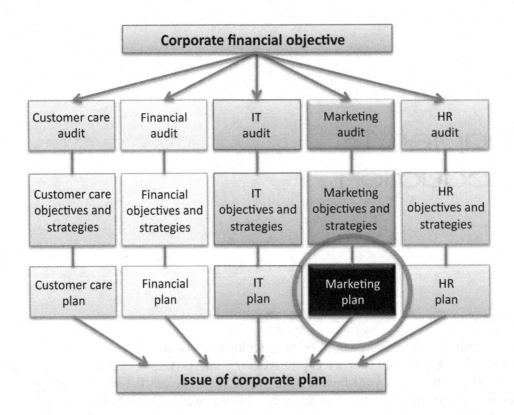

Marketing plan vs. others

10 Principles of Marketing Planning

Before you become acquainted with the various components of a marketing plan, it's important for you to understand the principles of marketing planning. Just skim through these 10 points and bear them in mind when you write your plan later.

1. Develop the high-level, strategic marketing plan first; the detailed operational plan is derived from this.

2. Put marketing as close as possible to the customer. If you're working for a multi-national corporation (MNC), empower your foreign subsidiary and channel to come up with the marketing plan because they are closer to the customers.

3. Marketing is an attitude from the customer's perspective; it is not a set of company procedures.

4. Organize activities around customer groups, not functional activities. Implication: you can have a cross-functional team with sales, customer care and marketing people working together to run a marketing event.

5. A marketing audit must be rigorous to reveal the truth. No vague terms should be allowed, and nothing should be hidden. The practice of "sandbagging" to adjust quarterly marketing numbers should be avoided.

6. The SWOT (strengths, weakness, opportunities, and threats) analysis should be focused on market segments that are critical to the business; concentrate only on key factors that lead to objectives. That is, there is no need to do a SWOT analysis on every segment that you serve.

7. If you're the boss, you must educate your staff on the planning process. On the other hand, if you're being tasked to write a marketing plan for your boss, you must be educated on the planning process. Do you have just a few days or up to a month to prepare the plan? Don't be afraid to ask your boss for clarification.

8. There has to be a plan for planning. For example, "I will spend a maximum of three days to plan the marketing planning process and then move on." Never have meeting after meeting just to talk about who are responsible for the marketing plan and how it should be written.

9. All objectives should be prioritized in terms of urgency and impact to return on investment (ROI) and/or customer satisfaction.

10. Marketing planning needs the active support of the chief executive and must be appropriate for the culture of the organization. Ask around. Is your boss asking you to write a plan simply for the sake of writing one? Will your plan be turned into actions later? Really?

Recipe for Writing a Strategic Marketing Plan

Some students spend about $100 to buy those marketing plan authoring software in the hope that such software can help them write the perfect plan using the least amount of time. Unfortunately, many students just get confused and disappointed. Many of these software use Q&A-type processes to help you put the plan together. Unfortunately, students often get "stuck" with certain questions and the serial writing process stops.

As a professor, I've reviewed hundreds of marketing plans a year written by my MBA students. Is there a perfect template for a marketing plan? No, I don't think so. It really depends on your industry, the size of your organization, and the reason for writing such a plan. If your boss doesn't have much time to study your masterpiece, perhaps a 7- to 10-page document with a great executive summary would be sufficient. Remember, it's not a competition to write the thickest marketing plan on earth. Who has the time and energy to go through your 300-page marketing plan?

As a rule of thumb, a marketing plan should cover the following 12 major areas:

1. Executive Summary

2. Introduction

3. Situational Analysis

4. Target Market

5. Competitive Analysis

6. Financial Analysis

7. Product Strategy

8. Pricing Strategy

9. Integrated Marketing Communications Strategy (Promotion)

10. Channels of Distribution Strategy (Place)

11. Resource Allocation and Monitoring

12. Conclusion

In Chapter 2, I will discuss each of these major sections in more detail.

Chapter 2 –
The 12-section Marketing Plan

Section (1): Executive Summary

The executive summary is a one-page synopsis of your entire marketing plan. It is an abstract of that which your boss is about to read, often on their Blackberries! In the executive summary, you should include:

- a measurable goal for your marketing plan and how your marketing plan's success will be evaluated in quantitative outcomes;

- a mission statement that is a standalone paragraph, which should state the business or industry your organization is operating in; and

- a brief paragraph that shares specifics about each of the sections that follows.

Don't forget that the executive summary is just a quick overview of your marketing plan, so there's no need to dig into the details here. When your reader is done reading the executive summary, he or she should say, "OK, now I know what this company does and what you want to accomplish with this marketing plan."

When writing the executive summary, make sure to include your financial highlights such as revenue forecasts, projected growth in unit sales, market share, and expected profitability. Briefly refer to the current market situation and how the recent changes (e.g., customer's shopping behavior, mergers and acquisitions (M&A) of the industry players, new government regulations, etc.) pose an opportunity for your product or service. Point out key success factors and/or major pitfalls you plan to avoid. Discuss major actions, changes, or trends that you anticipate over the planning period (e.g., the next three years), and how these will impact the marketing strategy that you are proposing.

I know you're tempted to write much more in this section, but try your best to keep it a one-pager. Don't worry if you've written a little bit more but never make it into three or more pages long!

Section (2): Introduction

This introductory section helps the readers quickly understand what you're trying to launch and the financial numbers that you are trying to achieve with your marketing plan.

First, start with a "mission statement" to show the reader what your organization is all about, as if you're talking to a stranger. Briefly mention where your company is headquartered and, if it's an MNC, the extent to which it is operating globally.

Then, describe for your reader what it is that you wish to bring to the market. If it is a product, describe the product, its functionality, and how it works. If it is a service, describe the service offering so that the reader understands what they would receive. Add a photo, diagram, or some basic drawings if the product or service is very unique to grasp the reader's attention.

When describing your product or service, (i) highlight the problem that it will solve, as perceived by the target market; (ii) show the competitive advantage that your product or service is offering; and (iii) discuss the challenges that you might face in the marketing of such product or service.

Make sure that you have adequately described your product or service. By the time the reader has completed reading the introduction, he or she should understand what you want to bring to the market. If you have a service description, the reader would know where your shop is located and what service is offered.

Wrap up the introductory with a "financial summary" to illustrate the revenue and profit projection for the full planning period. Add a line or bar graph if you can. Remember, VPs and directors love to see numbers!

Section (3): Situational Analysis

The major idea of the situational analysis is to educate the reader about the industry that you're operating in. Think about it: do you think a venture capitalist or a senior VP who is reviewing your marketing plan would know everything about your specific product and its market? No, they won't. The situational analysis section is the opportunity for you to show what's going on in the market place, and set the stage for the subsequent discussion to make it meaningful. Very often, this is the section in which the reader would say, "Ah...I don't realize that this market has gone through such changes in the past few years!"

Here, you should carry out a "market overview" to set the stage. Consider the following points as you begin to write this section:

- Market structure: What's the market and who are the players?
- Market trends: Has the market declined or grown?

- Key market segments: How does the market break down into customer segments? What are the trends in each of them?

There are many ways you can write your market overview. Many students often find it helpful to make use of academic frameworks such as SWOT analysis, product life cycle analysis, Ansoff matrix, and diffusion of innovation analysis to write their market overview. You can also perform a Gap analysis or a detailed marketing audit (see later sections) to explore the shortfall between the corporate objective and what can be achieved by various strategies.

Since the SWOT analysis is often included in the marketing plan these days, let me talk about it a little bit further. This analysis refers to analysis in the following four areas:

- S: "Strengths" that you bring to the market and that make you a formidable competitor.

- W: "Weaknesses" that you can identify and have to address, as your competition is aware of them and will likely exploit them to their advantage.

- O: Identify the "Opportunities" that allow you to capitalize on your strengths. Where might you grow your business in terms of market share, revenues, and profitability?

- T: Identify the "Threats" in the macro-environment. These include those aspects that you cannot control, but they are there – the economy, the competition, the political and legal environment. Are there any new laws and regulations that affect how your customers shop/buy/use/dispose of your product?

The SWOT analysis is usually written in bullet form, with each bullet not exceeding two lines. Try to list three to five bullet points under each heading (e.g., Strengths). Don't list a whopping 15 bullet points for Strengths but only 2 for Weaknesses. Make sure that your SWOT analysis is factual and non-fiction. You want to demonstrate your realistic assessment of the market environment.

If you are writing a marketing plan for your professor, or if your reader has a consulting or MBA background, it is also a good idea to utilize some academic theories and frameworks to supplement your analysis. These include Porter's 5-force model and/or P.E.S.T. (Political, Economic, Social, Technological) analysis. You can also choose to include them in the Appendix if your situational analysis section is already too long. Remember, there's no need to include all of these frameworks in your paper to show that you have done the homework. More is not better, especially if you just stick the tables there without relating the findings to your subsequent discussion. Top MBA students in my class like to write a line or two to conclude their findings after each analysis.

Before you wrap up this section of situational analysis, make a brief statement about the key issues that have to be addressed in the planning period. Go back to the "Weakness" section of your SWOT analysis if you need an idea about what to write. If your marketing plan covers several product lines, give a portfolio summary using tools like the Boston Consulting Group (BCG) matrix or directional policy matrix. Finally, to manage your readers' expectation, list all assumptions clearly to avoid any confusion. For example, your fiscal year may not end in December 31!

Section (4): Target Market

Once you've discussed the overall market environment, it's time to describe the customer segments that you are trying to target with your product or service. In the target market section, you should:

- Describe your target market. Is it a business (B2B) or consumer (B2C or C2C) market? Make good use of the segmentation variables such as demographics, psychographics, behavioral, geographies, or other segmentation criteria.

- Describe your reasons for selecting such target market(s). State why the mentioned market(s) is (are) attractive to you, as a marketer.

- Describe the target market in terms of its anticipated growth, revenue opportunities, and past performance. You can use a few line/bar charts to show the numbers.

In general, your proposed target market should be identifiable, measurable, sustainable, accessible, and reachable. Unless you are selling something that is very generic and is good for everybody, your segmentation should not be too generic.

If your organization is currently serving several customer segments, discuss whether you have different business objectives for each of them. For example, it is possible that you want to achieve a higher market share in customer segment "A", increase profitability in segment "B", and utilize a status-quo (i.e., no change) strategy for segment "C".

Section (5): Competitive Analysis

The goal of the competitive analysis section is to show your reader who else is competing against you in the market, and your likelihood for success. This is the opportunity to show people that you have done your homework in researching your competitors.

One of the major mistakes my MBA students commit is not putting sufficient effort into analyzing the competitors. Very often, students claim that their proposed products or services are very unique and not directly comparable. Don't forget, however, that you've got a substitute product or service out there! Here's a quick example. Let's say you are trying to sell an energy drink that is made of organic coffee beans, tastes like chocolate milk, and has refreshing bubbles in the bottle. Alright, there's no similar product on the market (yet) but consumers like me can still choose among regular ice coffee, carbonized soft drink, and other caffeine-filled beverages when shopping at the store. Your innovative product will be placed side by side other products on the shelf. Consumers have many choices and hence you have competitors!

So, how many competitors do you need to include in your analysis? In my opinion, you should list about two to five meaningful competitors in your product category. That is, don't list all competitors in your market. Select only the key ones that will mostly affect your sales.

For your selected competitors:

- Indicate why you selected them. Offer a SWOT analysis that focuses on the strengths and weaknesses of each competitor.

- Describe each company, its current market share, product offerings, financials (e.g., revenues, profitability), current positioning within the market, target market, recent development (e.g., any M&A activity? break-through product being launched?), and how they position themselves to the target market that you are trying to reach.

- Compare your product or service with that offered by the competition. How will you differentiate yours from that offered by the competition? Discuss why your target market would likely choose yours over that of the competition. If you don't have a differentiator, your target market won't see one either.

- Describe the likely market response from these competitors once you begin to make ample waves, assuming that you are entering a market in which competition already exists. For example, do you think the competitors will copy your idea and launch similar products or services? Will they drop their prices significantly to prevent you from entering the market? How will their response affect your sales and profitability projection?

Section (6): Financial Analysis

As a marketing professional, you need to justify your marketing activities, whether it's an advertising campaign or a new product development proposal. You achieve this by first having a good understanding of the financial impact of your marketing initiative and then presenting your financial analysis in a well-structured manner using an industry-acceptable framework.

In the financial analysis section, the first thing to show is sales (unit or customer) and revenue ($) forecasts. Then, illustrate ROI using the Net Present Value (NPV) method. Usually, this is carried out for three to five years, but some companies may choose to use a timeframe of, say, one year or even one quarter (three months). It really depends on the product life cycle of your proposed product or service. If I were you, I would ask around in the office and clarify this point with my boss, as I don't want to reinvent the wheel. If you absolutely have no idea, go with a projection period of three years. You also need to show how much market share you are expected to achieve with this plan.

To help management evaluate the feasibility of your marketing plan, a break-even (BE) analysis is often required. After all, nobody wants to invest in a new product or service that will only break even in 20 years' time! As a rule of thumb, if your project can break even in 18 months, that's really good already. Most marketing plans that I've reviewed suggest a break-even period of less than three years.

To polish up your work, it is always a good idea to include a sensitivity analysis to show how these forecasts will be changed under various market conditions (good, normal, bad). For example, increase your sales forecast by 25% in the good scenario and reduce it by 25% from the normal projection when the market conditions turn bad.

Overall, your financial analysis should consist of the following:

1. Break-even analysis

2. NPV analysis

3. Sensitivity analysis for good, normal and bad business scenarios

If you are presenting a marketing plan of your start-up operation to venture capitalists, discuss when your operation will turn EBITDA positive as well. The formula for EBITDA is "Revenue – Expenses (excluding interest, tax, depreciation, and amortization)". It is a non-GAAP (generally accepted accounting principles) way of showing the future potential profitability (i.e., net margins) of your operation. See your accounting textbook for details. If you're working for an MNC or don't need to raise money, just forget about this EBITDA thing.

Section (7): Product Strategy

After you've discussed the numbers, it's a good idea to quickly remind the reader about the marketing objectives that you want to achieve with the plan and put the subsequent discussions into perspective. Then, you formulate the strategy in the following few sections through the use of a marketing mix analysis. That is, you discuss the product, price, promotion, and place (channel) strategy for your product or service. Let's start with product. In some service industries such as banking and insurance, marketers like to call their intangible "services" as "products". To me, it's OK if you name this section as "Service Strategy" if you find it more suitable.

There are many things that you can write about in this product strategy section, including but not limited to:

- A detailed description of your proposed product and service, if it has not been sufficiently covered in the introduction section (e.g., show technical details);

- The strategic focus of your organization (e.g., change from chasing market share to profitability);

- Product mix adjustment (e.g., sell more of certain products to a particular customer segment due to change of demand);

- Product development (e.g., discuss what's coming down the pipe);

- Product deletion (e.g., issue end-of-life [EOL] status for certain products); and

- Market deletion (e.g., withdraw from a certain geographical market due to political instability or economic concerns).

Make reference to your findings in your earlier target market and competitive analysis sections to help justify your proposed product strategy. Never just state what you want to produce without making any justification.

Section (8): Pricing Strategy

In the pricing strategy section, you need to outline the price you intend to charge for your product or service. Here, you must:

- Demonstrate that your price allows reasonable profits in accordance with your strategy, taking in consideration of your fixed costs (FC), such as rents and utilities, and your variable costs (VC), such as materials costs and employee salaries that you have determined in an earlier section.

- Discuss your rationale for the pricing strategy selected. At the minimum, you can mention if your proposed product or service is following a skimming, penetration, or market pricing strategy. If you are selling a range of products in the same product category, how is the product line pricing being developed? Make good reference to the academic theories and frameworks as presented in this book.

- Discuss if a discount is available for your product or service. Any volume discounts or special pricing for members?

- Weigh your pricing strategy with the pricing currently offered by your competition. Consider how your proposed price fits into the target market and compares with the competition.

If you are using a channel of distribution (e.g., authorized dealers), describe the profitability and trade terms (e.g., 2/10net30) you will have with your channel members to ensure appropriate profit at their end so that they will want to promote your product.

If your product or service has a relatively short product life cycle (e.g., a few months to a year) it is also a great idea to show graphically how the pricing of your product evolves over the planning period. For the service sector, you will be showing how the average revenue per user (ARPU) will be changing on a monthly basis.

Section (9): Integrated Marketing Communications Strategy

Nowadays, many promotional campaigns are carried out in an integrated manner (i.e., same theme and message across online and offline marketing channels), so marketers like to use the term "integrated marketing communications" or IMC to describe their promotional activities.

In the discussion of your promotional strategy, you have to develop a well-defined "message" that is consistently communicated to your stakeholders (customers, sales channel, media, employees, etc.).

Your promotional plan should:

- Indicate if it follows a "push", "pull", or a combination of these strategies.

- Demonstrate an appropriate mix of advertising, public relations, sales promotion, direct marketing, and personal selling in both online and offline settings.

- Be specific. If you are suggesting the use of Internet technology for promotion, explicitly tell your reader how you are going to do that: e-mail, banner ads, advertorials, and/or social media tools such as Facebook, Twitter, and QQ.

- List up to three major objectives for your promotional approach. Outline these in terms of measurable tasks that you want to accomplish. For example, how many products are you going to sell additionally with the launch of such promotional campaign? If it's too early to observe an increase of sales, use other operational metrics such as increase in number of website or retail store visits during the promotional period. These objectives are important because your boss needs to evaluate your promotional activities based on these stated evaluation criteria.

- Describe each of your promotional activities that you envision as essential to ensure an integrated approach to promoting your product or service.

- Clearly outline your execution (rollout) plan, in accordance with the following format for any marketing expenditures:

  1. Weekly 1/2-page ads in the Globe and Mail newspaper @$8,250 for each placement. Advertisement is run each Saturday for two months, followed by publication during alternate weeks for another six months. Total Cost is $165,000. Print ads start June 1, 2011.

  2. Thirty-second radio spots on AM680, with three ads during morning drive time and two during evening drive time; ads to run five days each week for

first two months and alternate every other week for another six months. Total Cost: $180,000. Radio ads start July 1, 2011.

Depending on the level of ROI details that your boss is expecting, you may need to break down the measurable outcome by each promotional activity. Instead of saying "the whole campaign will bring in 6500 more shoppers", you may need to break down the numbers to point out that "the print ads will generate 3000 additional store visits while the radio ad will bring in 3500 more shoppers during the promotional period."

If you are planning to launch quite a bit of promotional activities, use a table to outline the various items just like this:

Objectives	Campaign Description	Date	Costs	Measurable Outcome
Increase store traffic	Print Ads - Globe and Mail	June 1, 2011 - January 31, 2012	$165K	3000 additional shoppers
Increase store traffic	Radio Ads - AM640	July 1, 2011 - February 29, 2012	$180K	3500 additional shoppers

Overview of Promotional Activity

In this way, your boss can easily compare your various marketing activities and select the ones that he or she likes in case you can't get the approval to run them all. Help your boss to make the trade-off decision because it's a rare situation in which your organization would have an unlimited budget for you to spend.

I think it's best to include a timeline or even a Gantt chart to show the reader what marketing activities are going to happen in the coming weeks and months. This is important because you may be missing out some key dates that you don't know about. Perhaps the tradeshow for this year has been postponed from May till July, or your company won't be able to carry out the same number of launch events like last year due to a budget cut. Remember, your boss knows something you don't know. By clearly showing the dates for these proposed marketing activities, your boss can easily spot the problematic initiatives and have you adjusted them quickly later.

In case you run out of good ideas, the best starting point is to do some benchmarking with your competitors and piggyback on their strategies. See what they are doing and what they are not spending money on. Of course, you should never just copy your competitor's promotional strategy because they may have a bigger pocket (i.e., a larger IMC budget) than you. If your company has been focusing on just a few promotional activities thus far (e.g., printing flyers or running trade shows), it may be a good time to explore newer tactics, such as leveraging the use of social media for promotion.

When drafting your promotional activities, you need to carefully think about how your target customers will react to your advertising message. You may need to plan ahead all of the logistics or else your promotional campaign will fail. For example, if you are driving shoppers to visit your store, you need to ensure you have stocked up the promotional items in the store in advance. If your call-to-action item is to have your prospects call your sales hotline, make sure you set up the 1-800 phone number properly and train the call center representatives. These can be separate items that cost your organization time, money, and resources. In some cases, you may need to include these activities in your plan because they will be coming from your marketing budget!

Overall, you must show a clear understanding of what you want your IMC strategy to do for you in terms of measurable outcomes. The plan has to make business sense in terms of ROI, given that you could easily spend millions of dollars to promote your product or service in theory.

When all is done, your boss should be able to understand what you are trying to promote, how/when/where/to whom it's being promoted, the cost of your campaign, and most importantly, the expected business outcomes.

Section (10): Channels of Distribution Strategy

This is the section where you discuss the "place" element of your proposed marketing mix of your product or service. Place, as you should know by now, simply refers to the distribution channels of your product or service. In writing this section, remember to consider the following aspects:

- The reasons for the channel structure you have selected. For example, have you considered the use of direct selling? Why or why not? What are the values of your channel partners/intermediaries, if any?

- How you will work with your channel partners to help them promote your product to the end-user or buyer, in terms of financial incentives (e.g., merchant development fund [MDF], flexible return policy, lenient trade terms, and staff training).

- How you will manufacture your product, warehouse it, and move the product to the next channel level.

- Everything about sales commissions: What's the amount? Do you charge per unit or is it a percentage of revenue? Do you have an escalating structure (i.e., the more they sell, the higher the sales commission rate)?

- Sales expectation: Do you have any weekly, monthly or quarterly sales quota that your channel partners need to meet? How is sales reporting to be done? Do you need any new tools to access the sales data? This is important because you need visibility to early sales success or failure in order to adjust your marketing strategy afterwards.

Unless you are adopting a pure direct selling model, you have to discuss the selection, compensation, training, and management of your sales staff in this section. If you are providing a service to your target market, you may be fulfilling the responsibilities of a direct channel service provider (e.g., hair salon or business consulting). In this case, describe how and where you will provide the proposed services that you will offer your target market.

Section (11): Resource Allocation and Monitoring

In the final part of the marketing plan, you have to show your resource requirements and discuss how your marketing program will be measured and reviewed. You will need three kinds of resources: people, money, and time.

— People

In this section, you have to estimate how many people are required to work throughout your marketing program during the pre-launch, launch, and post-launch phases. If you have a limited headcount, have you considered getting external help by hiring third-party contractors, seeking help from the channel, or even borrowing people from other departments or subsidiaries? Can your organization allocate a cross-functional team to work in your marketing project? If the sales and customer care people do not report to you directly, there's a good chance that they won't be able to help no matter how "free" or "relaxed" they seem to be while working in the office. Remember, your priority is not theirs.

— Money

Of course you need money to run the marketing programs, but you have to be specific in your request: (i) how much do you need, (ii) when do you need to pay the bills, and (iii) is it possible to adjust the budget if the marketing campaign becomes a success or failure?

Speaking of cost estimation, some marketers make the mistake of ignoring certain cost elements such as travel (meals, flights, car rental, hotels) and training (internal and external). Try to think of all incremental costs that you may need to spend in addition to the IMC budget that you have calculated earlier in your marketing plan.

Always check with your finance folks to understand your organization's financial planning practice. Trying to spend a lot of marketing dollars in Q1? That may not be a good idea if most of your sales are happening in Q4. How about payments? What is the cut-off date for your accountants to close the book for the fiscal year? Not every organization has its fiscal year ending in December 31, so don't take "common sense" for granted.

Point (iii) about budget adjustment is actually very important. Imagine that your marketing program is to give out free toys to stimulate sales. What if it's a great success and the toys are all gone only three days into your program? You just can't tell the kids, "Sorry, you should have come earlier" when your print advertisements for the week are still showing your promotion. Similarly, you need to prepare yourself to handle unforeseen adverse market condition. Let's say you are targeting North Americans to promote tourism in Britain. Your beautiful ads are out in the media and they are well received by the public. All of a sudden, however, air travel to Europe becomes a mess due to volcanic ash from Iceland. You need extra money to re-run your campaign later in the year when travelers are no longer afraid of flying to Britain.

To impress your boss, include a sensitivity analysis to show the good, expected, and bad scenarios. Don't spend three weeks to do your sensitivity analysis; a ball-park estimation using prior project experience will do. If you absolutely have no clue, use the following as a starting point in your discussion with your boss:

Good scenario: sales x 1.2, cost x 0.8
Expected scenario: sales x 1.0, cost x 1.0
Bad scenario: sales x 0.8, cost x 1.2

— Time

Another major problem is that marketers like to assume employees will dedicate 100% of their time to work on the proposed marketing activities. No, it won't happen even if an employee is assigned to work on your project only. People are multi-tasking all the time to deal with their personal and business issues, so it's not uncommon to observe scheduling problems. If you have ever worked as a project manager, you should know that unexpected things often happen in a project: People may get sick and need to take time off. Your external vendor may delay its job completion for whatever reasons. Even shipment of your goods to the retailers may be delayed. It is virtually impossible to accurately estimate the time required to run your project, so I strongly advise you to build a "buffer" in your plan (e.g., let's say you think the preparation needs 10 weeks, make it 11 weeks in your plan. That extra week is your buffering zone.)

— Documentation, Documentation, and Documentation

After talking about what kind of resources you need for your marketing initiatives, you have to show the management how your program will be reviewed and measured. There's an old saying, "Always document your success!"

In an MNC, a marketing program is always evaluated three months after it's implemented. If the marketing program is successful, the company may want to repeat it or give additional resources to achieve further success. On the other hand, if the program is not generating the expected result, it's best to have a review to identify the gap. Perhaps it's a great program but the chosen channel is not the right one, or there's a sudden change of external environment like the economic crisis that you could not have predicted earlier on. In those cases, your company may want to put a stop on your program to cut losses, or re-launch it after certain program adjustments. Without such evaluation, you may be wasting valuable marketing resources.

This kind of program review also forms the official evaluation of your own job performance. What if your boss leaves the company soon after you have completed this successful marketing campaign? You need evidence to show your new boss (and HR) that you are the one who successfully carried out this marketing plan. This kind of documentation also allows you to secure future budget and management approval if you plan to run similar marketing campaigns again later.

Section (12): Conclusion

For some bosses, marketing is viewed as a cost center that spends money. From their perspective, the less money marketing needs, the better. I'm not going to say whether this is good or not because each organization has its own challenges and culture. What I want to say is that you are writing a plan to "ask for money". A large company reviews many marketing plans a week. It should not be surprising to learn that your plan is being compared against 30 or more plans in the queue.

To get the company to prioritize resources to work on your marketing plan, you must persuade your boss (or the venture capitalist) that spending money with your proposed marketing activities is a good idea. The concluding section gives you the opportunity to paint a great picture of your plan. Highlight the key action items and their ROI in terms of revenue, profitability, and brand equity improvement. Clearly show what the company can expect in both the short term and the long term. Make good use of tables if required. Perhaps most importantly, you have to argue why this plan has to be approved without delay. Is there any sense of urgency? Discuss the consequences if this plan is not implemented, such as loss of market share, profitability, or potential growth of company value. In general, this section should not be more than one page long. It may be the only section that your boss reads (other than the executive summary), so make it a concise one that covers all of the key points.

Chapter 3 – Advanced Analytical Tools

In the next few pages, I'm going to show you some of the analytical tools that you may include in your marketing plan. Frankly speaking, the inclusion of these advanced tools only makes sense if your reader has an MBA or has worked in the financial or consulting sector previously. Otherwise, they may probably say, "What's that? Can you explain this concept?"

Marketing Audit

A marketing audit is usually made up of two sections: the external and the internal audits. In your external audit section, you can talk about how the "business and economic environment" is shaped by the following factors:

- Political / fiscal / legal
- Economic
- Social / cultural
- Technological
- Intra-company

Then, you can talk about your "market" in terms of its total market, size, growth, and trends (value/volume). You can briefly discuss the market characteristics by touching on the following areas:

- Products
- Prices
- Physical distribution

- Channels
- Customers / consumers
- Communication
- Industry practices

A marketing audit won't be complete if you don't discuss your competitors. There are many things that you can make reference to, such as:

- Name of major competitors
- Competitor size
- Market share / coverage
- Market standing / reputation
- Production capabilities
- Distribution policies
- Marketing methods
- Extent of diversification
- Personnel issues
- International issues
- Profitability
- Key strengths and weaknesses

The second part of your marketing audit focuses on the "internal" aspects, such as looking at how marketing has been performed in your organization. You can discuss:

- Sales (total, by location, by customer segment, by product line)
- Market share / coverage
- Profit margins / costs
- Marketing mix (4Ps)
- Overall operation and resource issues, if any

Gap Analysis

In a Gap Analysis, you identify the difference between your actual sales revenue and your expected one based on your corporate objective. To close this difference (gap), you discuss various strategic and tactical changes that you intend to make. Example strategies include:

- Having a new corporate objective (e.g., General Motors: focus on profitability and not market share);

- Having a new strategy (e.g., Apple: shift focus from the personal computer to the smartphone market);

- Diversification (e.g., Canadian Tires launches credit card and other banking services);

- Entering new markets (e.g., Tim Hortons expands to the USA);

- Launching new products;

- Focusing on market penetration (e.g., lower pricing for selected goods at Loblaws); and

- Enhancing productivity (e.g., launch of self-checkout kiosks at Home Depot and Loblaws).

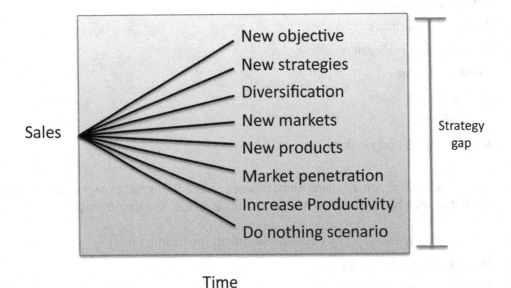

Strategy Gap

Remember that it is not necessary for you to make use of all these strategies. Pick the one(s) that you think make sense. You can also discuss why certain strategies should not be used; perhaps a similar competitor has tried such strategy and failed recently? The idea here is to close the strategy gap to meet your revenue and profitability expectation.

Porter's 5 Forces model

The Porter's 5 Forces model is often used as part of a situational (environmental) analysis. This model was created by Professor Michael Porter of Harvard in 1979. This model looks at five different areas:

1. Bargaining Power of Suppliers (e.g., Since the mid-2000s, major tire brands such as Michelin and Pirelli have stopped including "Road Hazards Damage Insurance" with the purchase of their new tires. When all of your favorite brands are doing the same thing at the same time, what else can you do as a consumer? Stop buying? Of course not!)

2. Bargaining Power of Customers (e.g., At Starbucks, instead of ordering just a cup of "Tall Bold", you can try the barista's skills by ordering a "grande hot decaf triple five-pump vanilla non-fat no foam whipped cream extra hot extra caramel upside down caramel machiatto!")

3. Threat of New Entrants (e.g., In 2010, new wireless entrants such as WindMobile, Mobilicity, Public Mobile, and a few others are joining the wireless market that was dominated by Bell, Telus, and Rogers.)

4. Threat of Substitute Products (e.g., Yes, people are not just buying Coke for the caffeine, they can now choose from a wide range of caffeine-filled products such as Red Bull, canned coffee, and all kinds of energy drinks.)

And these four aspects drive...

5. Competitive Rivalry within an Industry (i.e., you have to discuss whether the industry is competitive or not)

Students like to draw a diagram to show Porter's 5 Forces model. It's OK but not required in my opinion. The diagram looks like this:

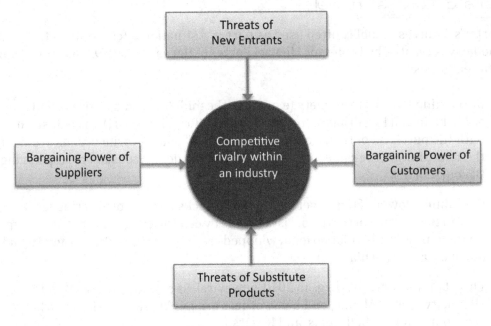

Porter's 5 Forces Model

Porter's Generic Competitive Matrix

Unlike Porter's 5 forces model, which is often used for situational analysis, his Generic Competitive Matrix, which consists of three strategies, is mainly used to describe how a business can achieve and maintain competitive advantage, based on its market scope and competency.

The three different kinds of generic strategies are:

- Segmentation Strategy (when you have a narrow market scope);
- Differentiation Strategy (when you have a broad market scope, and the company is able to produce unique products); and
- Cost Leadership Strategy (when you have a broad market scope, and the company is good at low-cost production).

While these strategies are not mutually exclusive, it is not common to see successful companies utilizing these strategies in a combined manner within a specific timeframe.

PEST Model

The P.E.S.T. Model is used in a situational analysis especially in an international marketing setting. There, you should talk about how political (P), economic (E), social (S), and technological (T) developments affect the market or industry that you are analyzing. Some professors don't like the "PEST" sound of this model and flip the letters around to call it the "STEP" Model or Framework, but they are the same. Other variations include SLEPT and STEEPLE but they are highly similar.

It is important to understand these developments. For example, it may not be a good idea to invest in countries like Iraq and Afghanistan due to their unstable political environment. Meanwhile, some countries are restricting access to certain Internet services (e.g., Skype) and social networking sites (e.g., Facebook, Twitter, Flickr), and you have to consider these limitations in your marketing plan. So, what can you write about the PEST? See some examples below:

— **Political (P)**
- Laws and regulations
- Tax policies
- Trade agreement
- Political Stability

— **Economic (E)**
- Economic growth
- Interest rates
- Unemployment policy
- Inflation rate

— **Social (S)**
- Demographics [age, ethnic, gender]
- Lifestyle change
- Education
- Living conditions

— **Technological (T)**
- Energy use and costs
- Mobile Technology Penetration

- Internet Uses
- Life cycle and speed of technological obsolescence

Key Success Factors (KSFs) Matrix

What are the few key things from the customers' point of view that any competitor has to do right to succeed? Your job is to identify these factors through research (e.g., survey, focus group) and give them weights. For example, let's say we are building a KSFs Matrix for a laptop and believe that the following four factors are important when customers are making their laptop purchase decisions:

Factors (Weight):
Price (50%)
Warranty (25%)
Battery Hours (20%)
CPU Speed (5%)

Then, you create a table to compare your product against the competitors, based on these evaluation criteria. Score your brand and each of your main competitors out of 10 (the best) on each of the KSFs, and then multiply the score by the weights. Sum them up to calculate the weighted score.

	Price (50%)	Warranty (25%)	Battery Hours (20%)	CPU Speed (5%)	Weighted Score
Your Brand	5	7	6	9	5.9
Competitor A	3	5	6	8	4.4
Competitor B	4	5	6	7	4.8
Competitor C	7	6	5	2	6.1
Competitor D	7	6	4	3	6.0
Competitor E	10	7	2	1	7.2

Key Success Factors Matrix

From this KSFs Matrix, you can see that your brand uses a fast CPU chip (hence a score of 9) but that does not help you too much because CPU chip only makes up 5% of the weighted score. The matrix also shows that your price is less competitive than those of Competitors

C, D, and E. As a result, the suggestion is to lower the price of your laptop by including a less expensive CPU chip because customers do not care too much about CPU speed.

Boston Consulting Group (BCG) Matrix

The Boston Consulting Group Matrix is also known as the BCG Matrix or the Boston Matrix. It was developed in 1968 through a BCG perspective titled "The Product Portfolio". The BCG Matrix is useful in product portfolio planning as it classifies a firm's product into one of four categories, namely:

- Star (high market share, high market growth potential);
- Cash Cow (high market share, low market growth potential);
- Question Mark (low market share, high market growth potential); and
- Dog (low market share, low market growth potential).

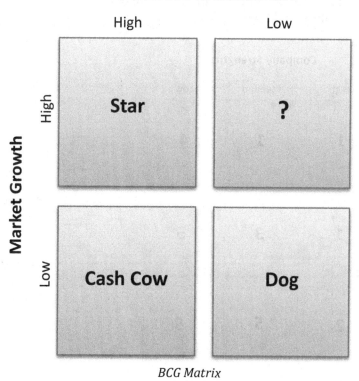

BCG Matrix

Adapted from: http://www.bcg.com/about_bcg/history/history_1968.aspx

In general, a company should direct most resources to promote products (or services) that belong to the "Star" category. Meanwhile, a company should not invest additional resources to promote those "Cash Cow" products because the goal is to "milk" these products for profits at minimal costs. Products like DVD players are cash-cow products that have reached maturity stage but there is still a lot of demand in the market, so they should just be made at low cost, without spending R&D or advertising dollars on this product. For example, you may no longer need to have a dedicated product manager looking after the DVD player line.

For those questionable products that seem to have huge market potential but little success in market acceptance, perhaps you can sell them to other companies before it's too late, or carry out additional research before re-launching them. Finally, "Dog" products should be eliminated as they contribute little to your overall product portfolio. However, some companies keep these doggy products because they are part of a bigger "solution" for key clients and hence they should not be viewed in an isolated manner.

Directional Policy Matrix (DPM)

General Electric developed the Directional Policy Matrix (DPM) during the 1970s. It is also known as the GE Matrix, or the GE Multi-factor Model. Instead of having four quadrants, DPM has a 3x3 matrix and looks like this:

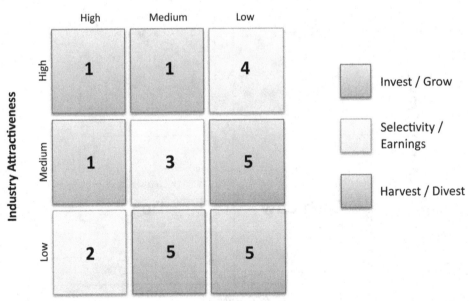

Directional Policy Matrix

By placing your products (or services) into one of these nine blocks, you can fit your product to use one of the following five business strategies.

— 1. Invest for Growth:

Market share: Maintain or increase dominance
Products: Differentiations - line expansion
Price: Lead - aggressive pricing for share
Promotion: Aggressive marketing
Distribution: Broaden distribution
Cost control: Tight control - go for scale economies
Production: Expand, invest (organic acquisition, joint venture)
R&D: Expand - invest
Personnel: Upgrade management in key functional areas
Investment: Fund growth
Working capital: Reduce in process - extend credits

— 2. Maintain market position, manage for earnings:

Market share: Maintain or slightly milk for earnings
Products: Eliminate less successful ones, differentiate for segments
Price: Stabilize prices/raise
Promotion: Limit
Distribution: Hold wide distribution pattern
Cost control: Emphasize cost reduction
Production: Maximize capacity utilization
R&D: Focus on specific projects
Personnel: Maintain, reward efficiency, tighten organization
Investment: Limit fixed investment
Working capital: Tighten credit - reduce accounts receivable, increase inventory turnover

— 3. Selective

Market share: Maintain selectivity - segment
Products: Emphasize product quality
Price: Maintain or raise
Promotion: Maintain selectively
Distribution: Segment
Cost control: Tight control
Production: Increase productivity (e.g. specialization)
R&D: Invest selectively
Personnel: Allocate key managers
Investment: Invest selectively
Working capital: Reduce

— 4. Opportunistic development

> Market share: Invest selectively in share
> Products: Differentiation - line expansion
> Price: Aggressive - price for share
> Promotion: Aggressive marketing
> Distribution: Limited coverage
> Cost control: Tight - but not at expense of entrepreneurship
> Production: Invest
> R&D: Invest
> Personnel: Invest
> Investment: Fund growth
> Working capital: Invest

— 5. Manage for cash

> Market share: Forego share for profit
> Products: Aggressively eliminate obsolete ones
> Price: Raise
> Promotion: Minimize
> Distribution: Gradually withdraw/reduce distribution
> Cost control: Aggressively reduce fixed and variable costs
> Production: Free up capacity
> R&D: None
> Personnel: Cut back organization
> Investment: Minimize and divest opportunistically
> Working capital: Aggressively reduce

Ansoff Matrix

Professor Igor Ansoff in 1957 proposed a framework to help organizations to decide their growth strategy and understand their associated risks. This framework can be presented in the following 2x2 matrix, which is now known as the "Ansoff Matrix":

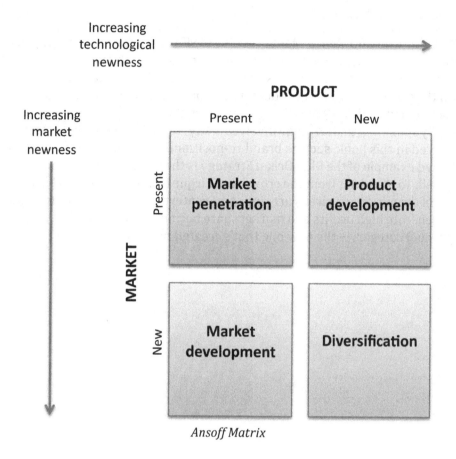

Ansoff Matrix

In simple terms, Ansoff suggests that there are four strategies that a company can use to grow its business:

1. **Market Penetration** (use your existing products to penetrate existing market) E.g. Advertise the George Brown College program in the Greater Toronto Area.

2. **Market Development** (promote your existing products in new markets) E.g. Launch the Queen's Executive MBA program in Ottawa.

3. **Product Development** (develop new products for your existing market) E.g. Launch Primus the Hybrid car for people who like to drive Japanese cars.

4. **Diversification** (develop new products and sell them in new markets) E.g. HP moved from an "Imaging and Printing" business to include a wide range of products and services such as Services, Personal Systems, Enterprise Storage and Servers, and HP Software. Its acquisition of Palm in 2010 is an example of its diversification strategy to expand into the smartphone and software business.

Blue Ocean Strategy

In 2005, W. Chan Kim and Renée Mauborgne of INSEAD proposed a strategy called "Blue Ocean" which basically suggests that companies create new demand in an "uncontested market space" to avoid competition. In simple English, the Blue Ocean Strategy asks you to break down the traditional wall of product definition, re-think how your product or service should be positioned, and come up with new products by thinking out of the box.

Technically speaking, this strategy involves many well-known strategies and tactics that we have covered in this book, such as brand re-positioning and product differentiation.

A well-cited example of the Blue Ocean Strategy is the Canadian entertainment company Cirque du Soleil. To stand out from the crowd, the Cirque du Soleil show can be described as a combination of drama, opera, circus art, and street entertainment. Its uniqueness allows the company to generate high profits and market share because there isn't a direct competitor in the same product category – the new one that's created by Cirque du Soleil.

Chapter 4 –
Marketing Plan Example –
Consumer Services

Restaurant

Highlights of this Marketing Plan:
1. A well-balanced plan
2. Comprehensive discussion on IMC strategy
3. Detailed financials presented in the Appendix

Executive Summary
ASFCN Seafood & Steakhouse will open the eyes of the residents of New York, NY and surrounding communities. It is a new restaurant that will bring the best of the local community together and will give back to the community just as much as it takes in.

Mission Statement
We are committed to providing only the best in local food and entertainment with a knowledgably and enthusiastic wait-staff. Our desire is to offer a rewarding dining experience in a comfortable, casual and relaxing atmosphere. We strive to better the quality of life of all local residents by providing a welcoming environment that encourages those in the community to come and share time together.

The ASFCN Restaurant will offer the finest choices in meat and seafood brought in from local suppliers already well known and respected in the community. It will provide an opportunity for these businesses to grow while at the same time helping to keep restaurant expenses lower due to the experience these local suppliers bring.

Objectives

1. Sales of over $1.5 million in the first year

2. To achieve growth of 10% in each of the first two years of operation

3. Profitable in year #3

Financials

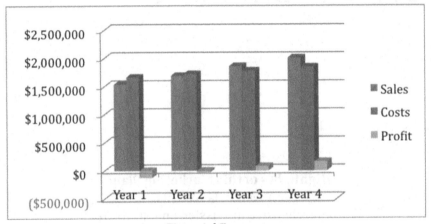

Financial Forecast

Service Description – Full Service Restaurant

I propose to bring to market a full-service restaurant to the New York area. This restaurant will have a different twist and bring something new to the area. It will succeed in recessionary times as well as when the economy is flourishing by being flexible and able to adapt to changing trends. Partnerships with established local businesses will bring trusted local expertise to the restaurant and a feeling from the restaurants patrons that they are helping their local community by supporting local businesses.

Trend

In keeping with the local theme, locally grown produce and meats will be used to the greatest extent economically possible. According to FranchiseDirect.com and the National Restaurant Association, the use of local products by a restaurant is becoming more and more popular among customers seeking out dining experiences.

*It is projected that in 2010 consumers will be interested in **locally produced and sourced food**. According to the National Restaurant Association 70% of adult consumers said that they are more likely to visit a restaurant that offers locally produced food items. The trend of locally sourced foods has become particularly popular at fine-dining establishments. According to the National Restaurant Association's research, **89% of fine-dining operators serve locally sourced items**, and 9 in 10 believe demand for locally sourced items will grow in their segment in the future. (2010)*

Local food and drink will not be the only "local" products offered by the ASFCN Restaurant. Local entertainment will be sought out and given an opportunity to showcase their talents on specially advertised evenings.

Highlights

- *Meat market* – A partnership with a local, already established butcher shop called ABC Meats will be made and space in the entryway of the restaurant will be available for customers to make purchases whether or not they patronize the restaurant. All meat used by the restaurant will be purchased from this butcher shop.

- *Seafood market* – A partnership with a local, already established seafood wholesaler, ABC Fish, will be made and space in the entryway of the restaurant will be available for customers to make purchases whether or not they patronize the restaurant. All seafood used by the restaurant will be purchased from this seafood supplier.

- *"Themed" dining areas* – There will be a general dining area for families with children, a sports bar/lounge, and a formal dining room with more of a quiet, romantic setting reserved for couples/adults only.

- *Community garden* – A partnership with a local farm will be made and land next to the restaurant will be reserved for local residents to grow their own vegetables. Any produce required from the restaurant, will first come from the community garden and the partnered farm. The chief chef and farm managers will be available to assist residents with their garden questions and needs.

- *Complimentary services* - Babysitting, valet, and taxi services will be made easily available at (sometimes at no charge) to encourage use and attract customers.

The restaurant will be geared around relaxation. Today's world is a very busy and stressful one. People need a place in which they can unwind, loosen up, and just enjoy each other's company. Most restaurants only do one thing – serve food. The ASFCN takes it to the next level and beyond. Salt water ASFCNs with tropical fish will be built into many walls to help create an atmosphere of calm and tranquility. Advertising for the restaurant will portray real people, in real day-to-day stressful situations. The viewer will be able to relate to the person in the advertisement and say "I know just how he/she feels." The advertisements would always end showing these same individuals in a relaxing setting and enjoying the company of others - similar to the old 1980's *Calgon* "take me away" television commercials.

SWOT Analysis

Strengths

- Wide range of entertainment options
- Partnerships with local established businesses
- Convenience, easy to get to location
- Customer service, food quality & atmosphere
- Recession proof
- Large community presence
- Environmentally conscious
- Six Sigma Enterprise

Weaknesses

- Broad range of services (spread too thin?)
- Customer service training requirements
- Use of university culinary students
- New restaurant to the area – will have to build customer loyalty from the ground up

Opportunities

- Opening up more community involvement
- Downtown economic expansion
- Roadway expansion project will soon force nearby restaurant to close its doors
- Location has close proximity to movie theater
- Using VoC (Voice of the Customer) to always come up with innovative new options for patrons

Threats

- Competition from nearby restaurants
- Competition from nearby supermarkets (meat & seafood suppliers)
- High local Real Estate & NY State Room & Meals taxes
- Fluctuations in beef and seafood costs

Target Market

The target market for this restaurant is based on a combination of behavioral (benefit & occasion) and psychographic segmentation. The primary consumer we want to reach range in ages from 21 to 65. They are working, single or married (with or without children), middle to upper class, are interested in quality food and drink coupled with leisurely activities in a comfortable setting.

Behavioral "Benefit" Segmentation:

Benefits to the consumer vary depending on the restaurant service they select. For those dining in the family setting, convenience and menu choices will be priority number one. Low-cost options and "kids eat free nights" will be available to those on tight budgets. Those choosing to dine in the elegant, fine dining room will enjoy an atmosphere and food quality normally found only in larger metropolitan settings. New consumers will automatically receive reward key-tags with credits based on the amount of their purchase, which can then be later redeemed at the restaurant or participating local merchants (i.e. Movie Theater) as an incentive to come back often.

Behavioral "Occasion" Segmentation

This consumer market is more apt to have a reason to "want to get away" from the everyday grind. Holidays such as Mother's Day & St. Patrick's Day, or birthdays and anniversaries give the public a reason to want to go out and celebrate. Weekend evenings are popular times for people to unwind from a long workweek.

Psychographic Segmentation

Consumers that are in the upper-middle to upper class will be attracted to the fine dining and classical atmosphere. Special evenings of ball-room dancing and/or live piano music will keep them coming back for more. Younger working-class adults will enjoy the sports lounge and social setting that allows them to meet others of the same age and tastes. Live entertainment, including local bands and comedy nights, will raise interests and cater to a blend of different lifestyles which will provide a reason to return over and over again.

These market segments are attractive because these would-be patrons (1) have cash to spend and (2) a need to de-stress in order to improve their quality of life.

Competitive Analysis

The New York area has many restaurant choices for consumers. Most are in the form of casual, quick service, "not-too-fancy" style restaurants. Two restaurants in nearby Manhattan will be primary competitors. These are CDE Restaurant and FGH Italian Grille. Both of these fine dining establishments offer more than just food, which make them very similar to the new restaurant.

CDE Restaurant

CDE Restaurant has live entertainment each Friday and Saturday night, a popular "Pub at CDE Restaurant" lounge to relax and watch your favorite sports team, and a banquet center which can host wedding receptions, corporate events, or private parties. CDE Restaurant is well known for its "award winning" prime rib, which will compete directly with the new restaurants fresh "butcher counter" meat dinner selections. It also offers popular seafood dishes and a large salad bar.

Location: (about 6 miles from ASFCN restaurant)
123 Main Road
New York, NY 012345-2345

SWOT analysis for CDE Restaurant:

- **Strengths**
  - Close proximity to the International Airport
  - Ideal setup for business functions
  - Well established and popular following
- **Weaknesses**
  - Food considered just average
  - Limited size for dining services
- **Opportunities**
  - Industrial park expansion
  - Catering services
- **Threats**
  - Many competing area restaurants
  - Airport hotels increasing competition for business seminars/events

FGH Italian Grille

FGH serves and is known for its many great Italian dishes, but will also keep customers coming back for their favorite steak and seafood dishes as well. The atmosphere is casual and relaxing and is situated in a renovated mill building (old shoe factory). It is ideally located near many businesses as well as residential condominiums. *FGH* offers live entertainment every Friday & Saturday as well as Jazz and Blues nights during the week. Banquets, weddings, and business functions can all be held at this location.

Location: (about 15 miles from the ASFCN restaurant)
234 Johnston Street
New York, NY 01234-1234

SWOT analysis for FGH Italian Grille:
- Strengths
- Long time in business (established restaurant)
- Owner operates multiple restaurants throughout the State
- Excellent food quality
- Good location to downtown New York
- Weaknesses
- Limited space resulting in a "cramped" feeling
- Open concept leads to noisy environment
- Opportunities
- Take out and catering services expansion
- Threats
- Many competing restaurants

Other competing area restaurants

- Bus Stop Restaurant
- Mr. Hungry Restaurant
- The Best Steakhouse
- Tommy Pizza & Restaurant
- Jimmy's Italian Place

Differentiator

ASFCN Seafood & Steakhouse will differentiate itself from the competition through more community involvement and beyond just restaurant services. Valet service during busy times and onsite babysitting will be available. Wait staff will be professionally trained and patron's orders will be communicated directly to the kitchen through hand-held PDAs to ensure accuracy and timeliness for preparing meals.

The new restaurant will also be a closer option to those in the immediate Manhattan area that do not want to travel further to the often-congested Manhattan infrastructure. Live entertainment will include "home grown" bands and comedy performances. During the summer months, an outdoor concert series with free admission to an outdoor viewing area will be planned on a biweekly basis.

The restaurant will have a "Birthday Program" to entice customers to come dine on their birthdays with friends and family. "Research shows that 50 percent of all Americans eat out on their birthday.° This program will be a good way to capture this part of the market.

Financial Analysis

The ASFCN restaurant will not be profitable until year three. It will take at least the first two years to get established and build on its brand. The restaurant will meet its financial obligations by securing bank loans. A detailed 4-year projected operating cost statement has been included in Appendix D.

Prime Cost

Prime cost is "one of the most telling numbers on any restaurant's P&L." For a full service restaurant, this figure should be 65% or less. Prime cost is the total cost of sales less payroll expenses and it is a means to accurately measuring the restaurant's performance. A percentage higher than 65% could indicate that sales are not high enough to support the hired help or that there are scheduling problems.

The *Prime Cost* for the ASFCN Restaurant in its first year will be approximately 72.4% which is higher than we want in the long run, but necessary as we start out. The reasoning is that prices will be kept low for the first couple years as we gain market share. This metric will come down in following years as the restaurant becomes profitable.

Controllable Profit

Another key number watched by those in the restaurant industry is that of *Controllable Profit*. How well a restaurant is being managed can often be told by this metric as this number is derived by only those items that management has influence and control. Typical for a full-service restaurant is a value from 15% to 20%.

The *Controllable Profit* for the ASFCN Restaurant in its first year will be approximately 7.1% followed by 12.3% in the second year. Again, these percentages are not in the desired acceptable range but are expected to rise once the restaurant is established.

Sales growth in years two and three are expected to reach 10% before stabilizing at 8% in year four. Profits will be realized in year three.

Product Pricing Structure

As described in the Part #2 (Service Description), there will be three distinct areas of the restaurant. Each of the three areas will have a different pricing scheme as described below. Also see Appendix D for the 4-Year Operating Projections.

Family Dining Room

The pricing strategy here is one of survival. Prices will be kept as low as possible during the first two years in order to get the consumer to come in and then coming back. The average cost of a meal will be $10 - $14, soft drinks will have free refills and prices for alcoholic beverages will be average for the dining industry.

Sports Bar/Lounge

The pricing strategy in the bar/lounge will be one of "maximum current profit". Special drink nights including $1 drafts will be scheduled on set nights to encourage customers to come in during low volume times.

Formal Dining Room

A "product-quality leadership" approach will be used in the adult's only dining room. Dining in the fine dining room will be an "affordable luxury" and more expensive but attractive due to the atmosphere and level of service, which will be top-notch - a value for which the customer will gladly pay extra. To start, through, the prices will still be slightly lower than plan until the restaurant gets established.

Channels of Distribution

The ASFCN Seafood & Steakhouse Restaurant will serve the greater New York, NY area through a newly built state-of-the-art dining facility. The location of the restaurant is minutes from downtown Manhattan. See Appendix C for physical location.

The layout of the dining facility will be split into three primary dining areas, a large entrance area including a butcher shop meat market and a seafood counter, a children's play area & babysitting service room, and of course the kitchen area. The kitchen will be situated in the middle of the building in order to have quick access to each area and also to serve as a noise buffer to help prevent noise from spilling from one dining area to another. An outdoor seating area will be available off the formal dining area and the sports bar/lounge for use during good weather. See Appendix F for the restaurant floor plan.

Professionally trained wait staff will use PDAs to enter patron orders that will be transmitted directly to the kitchen as soon as it is entered. Nightly specials and notifications of menu items that are not available (in cases where food has run out), can also be displayed directly on the PDA so that the wait staff is kept continuously informed.

Integrated Marketing Communication (IMC)

In order to reach out to the target customer, a mix of different promotional activities will be used. The restaurant is primarily concerned with reaching customers that reside in the New York Highway A-123 corridor. Print advertising in form of free publications, morning "drive-to-work" time radio commercials, evening news hour video advertising on local television stations, and public relations campaigns will be the core focus of communicating to customers. Included in these approaches will be birthday and holiday promotions, hosting business socials, specialty food and wine festivals, wedding/anniversary banquets, and charitable events.

Internet

A website will be created which will describe the restaurant and provide pictures of the dining areas. A full menu will be viewable and an online option to setup an account and put in for a reservation. A 5% discount will automatically be applied to all checks for patrons that make a same-day dinner reservation in the fine dining room.

Print

HGI Publishing LLC produces three weekly newspapers which are mailed and distributed free of charge to the community including every home in the towns of Manhattan and surrounding communities. This will be the primary advertising method along with television for the first year of operation. Advertising rates are very attractive and the publication reaches a large portion of the community.

Television

Channel 8 and Channel 10 will be the two local television stations chosen to air commercials to attract new customers and inform them of the amenities available with the new restaurant. Both stations are popular in the New York area and each serves a different demographic segment. Initially, as the restaurant gets off the ground, television advertising will be key to quickly getting images in the minds of potential customers.

CHANNEL 8

Manchester New Hampshire's CHANNEL 8 channel 9, an ABC affiliate, has been delivering the local and national news since 1954. Its slogan is *No One Covers New York Like We Do.* For anyone interested in learning the current weather forecast or what's happening in communities throughout the state, CHANNEL 8's newscasts are must watch TV.

For the restaurant, this makes it an ideal media advertising option during the 5:30 to 6:30 pm news hour. The likely audience is those that have recently returned home from work and are contemplating what to make for dinner. Setting the seed with a well-timed, 30-second commercial, may not get them in the restaurant's seats that evening but could very well do so in the days or weeks to follow. This type of customer will also tend to be older (over 35), more sophisticated, and middle to upper income.

CHANNEL 10

In 2005, the current ownership of CHANNEL 10-TV, a *BCDE TV* affiliate, took control of the former station Channel 7, a popular television station and favorite advertising medium for businesses since it started broadcasting in 1983. Since taking over, CHANNEL 10-TV, with its signature "My Super TV" branding, has continued to attract local businesses to advertise their products and services. The restaurant location will be less than one mile from the station's main office which means having a close B2B relationship will be important to get the word out in the initial year of operation.

CHANNEL 10-TV's programming philosophy is to focus on popular syndicated shows and its "My Super TV" brand while doing away with the news and weather broadcasting. This suggests a younger (under 40) audience, earning a middle to lower income salary, that is more interested in being entertained by a television sitcom rather than watching the news and following political events. This plays well with the get out, unwind and relax message the restaurant is trying to convey. The station also has a "My Favorite Restaurant" section on its website. Stay tuned for the new video soon to be released.

Television advertising is only expected to play a big part of the total advertising plan in the first year of business. After this time it is expected that the restaurant's brand will be well established and recognized in the surrounding community. Print and radio advertisements will continue on a continuous basis and may be enhanced as the more expensive television marketing is reduced. Television advertisement in the form of public relation campaigns will be more prominent in subsequent years.

Radio
Advertising on the radio will not be a major focus of this restaurant, but occasional advertising during the morning rush hour will be used in order to get the local community aware of the restaurant and where it is located.

WABC
WABC 89.7 claims to have *The Best Variety of Yesterday and Today* and, too many of their listeners, that would be an accurate assessment. Many commuters will have 89.7 tuned in on their FM radio dial while at home, driving the kids to school, or on the way to work in order to keep up with traffic updates. These morning commutes are a good time to offer up a suggestive commercial on what the new restaurant has available.

Public Relations
Much of the restaurant's theme is on being "green" and being "community friendly" by using

locally grown fruits and vegetables, meats and dairy from local farms, seafood caught or raised from local waters, and homegrown local talent for entertainment. Programs such as the community garden and free-to-the-public seminars on topics from bee keeping to growing zucchini, will keep local media coming back to report on the latest happenings. The restaurant will also host special events with some including VIP's, celebrities, or comedians, that will create a "buzz" around the community *and* the restaurant which will bring out the media.

The restaurant will host many food events. According to QMG, food events are:

> *a great way to position your restaurant as a center of the food scene in your market. It allows you to leverage the reputation, profile and credibility of all of the other participants, and it can also help you share the expense of holding the event. Hosting an event also provides your restaurant with the opportunity to recruit additional manpower and resources for promoting the event and gives that added edge with garnering local publicity.*

IMC Budget (Year 1)

Internet
A family member, and expert in website design and maintenance, will create an interactive website for the restaurant. Costs will be just over $3,000.

Print
Print advertising with HGI Publishing LLC will account for 60% of the IMC Budget in Year 1. Costs will be $28.6K in this first year. A full-size (half page) advertisement will be included in three community newspapers which are delivered free of charge on a weekly basis to 32,500 homes in Manhattan and other surrounding communities.

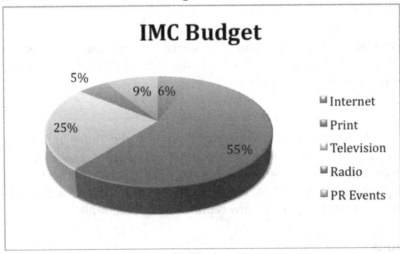

IMC Budget

Television

25% of the IMC budget will be spent on television advertisement with CHANNEL 8 and CHANNEL 10. Each station will produce a simple 30-second advertisement and air it in the morning and evening news hour (CHANNEL 8) and during evening sitcoms (CHANNEL 10). The average cost for each commercial aired, including production costs, will be $50. Budgeted dollars will allow for approximately 260 commercials to be aired. Patrons will be polled to see where they heard of the restaurant and commercial timing will be continuously adjusted throughout the first year.

Radio

Advertizing on WABC will only account for 5% of the IMC Budget. This will cover the production costs of a short 15-second commercial and air time on Friday mornings.

Public Relations Events

About $4,500 is set aside to be used for expenses associated with the restaurant's grand opening and other PR events.

Appendix D:

ASFCN Seafood & Steakhouse
4-Year Operating Projections
(Restaurant Profit Tools, 2009)

	Year 1	% Sales	Year 2	% Sales	Year 3	% Sales	Year 4	% Sales
Sales:	$		$		$		$	
Food	1,139,500		1,253,450		1,378,795		1,489,099	
Beverage	398,000		437,800		481,580		520,106	
TOTAL SALES	1,537,500		1,691,250		1,860,375		2,009,205	
Cost of Sales:								
Food	429,000		446,160		464,006		482,567	
Beverage	103,000		107,120		111,405		115,861	
TOTAL COST OF SALES	532,000	34.6%	553,280	32.7%	575,411	30.9%	598,428	29.8%
Gross Profit	1,005,500		1,137,970		1,284,964		1,410,777	
Payroll:								
Salaries & Wages	475,650		494,676		514,463		535,042	
Employee Benefits	105,900		110,136		114,541		119,123	
TOTAL PAYROLL	581,550		604,812		629,004		654,165	
PRIME COST	1,113,550	72.4%	1,158,092	68.5%	1,204,416	64.7%	1,252,592	62.3%
Other Controllable Expenses:								
Direct Operating Expenses	95,500		98,365		101,316		104,355	
Music & Entertainment	5,500		5,665		5,835		6,010	
Marketing	52,000		53,560		55,167		56,822	
Utilities	48,000		49,440		50,923		52,451	
General & Admin. Expenses	102,000		105,060		108,212		111,458	
Repairs & Maintenance	12,000		12,360		12,731		13,113	
TOTAL OTHER CONT. EXP.	315,000		324,450		334,184		344,209	
CONTROLLABLE PROFIT	108,950	7.1%	208,708	12.3%	321,776	17.3%	412,404	20.5%
Occupancy Costs & Depreciation								
Occupancy Costs	151,712	9.9%	154,746	9.1%	157,841	8.5%	160,998	8.0%
Depreciation & Amortization	81,038		81,038		81,038		81,038	
Other (Income) Expenses								
Other (Income)	(4,800)		(4,944)		(5,092)		(5,245)	
Interest Expense	52,547		47,292		42,563		38,307	
Other Expense	2,400		2,472		2,546		2,623	
NET INCOME BEFORE INCOME TAXES	(173,947)	11.3%	(71,897)	-4.3%	42,880	2.3%	134,683	6.7%
ADD BACK: Depreciation & Amortization	81,038		81,038		81,038		81,038	
DEDUCT: Loan Principle Payments	(35,105)		(38,780)		(44,117)		(53,200)	
CASH FLOW BEFORE INCOME TAXES	(128,014)	-8.3%	(29,639)	-1.8%	79,801	4.3%	162,521	8.1%

4-Year Operating Projection

Appendix E:

ASFCN Seafood & Steakhouse
CASH FLOW Break-Even Worksheet
(Restaurant Profit Tools, 2009)

Fixed Costs	Annual	Monthly
Total Management Salaries	$ 200,000	$ 16,667
Minimum Hourly Labor	$ 269,018	$ 22,418
Employee Benefits	$ 105,900	$ 8,825
Direct Operating Expenses	$ 74,824	$ 6,235
Music & Entertainment	$ 5,500	$ 458
Marketing	$ 52,000	$ 4,333
Utilities	$ 48,000	$ 4,000
General & Administrative	$ 102,000	$ 8,500
Repairs & Maintenance	$ 12,000	$ 1,000
Occupancy Costs:	$ 151,712	$ 12,643
Interest	$ 52,547	$ 4,379
Misc Other Expense	$ 2,400	$ 200
Loan Principle Payments	$ 35,105	$ 2,925
	$ 1,111,006	$ 92,584

Variable Costs	% of Sales	$
Cost of Sales	34.6%	$ 56,802
Hourly Labor	5.1%	$ 8,372
Employee Benefits	0.8%	$ 1,313
Credit Card Expense	2.0%	$ 3,283
Paper Supplies	1.1%	$ 1,806
	43.6%	$ 71,577

	Annual	Monthly	Weekly
Break-even Sales	$ 1,969,926	$ 164,160	$ 37,883

		Annual	Monthly	Weekly
Sales Break-Down:				
	Food	$ 1,181,955	$ 98,496	$ 22,730
	Liquor	$ 196,993	$ 16,416	$ 3,788
	Beer	$ 246,241	$ 20,520	$ 4,735
	Wine	$ 344,737	$ 28,728	$ 6,630
Total		$ 1,969,926	$ 164,160	$ 37,883

Break-Even Analysis

Break-Even Analysis Charts
    Average Sale/Cust. = $100.00
    Variable Costs =   43.60%
    CM = $56.40

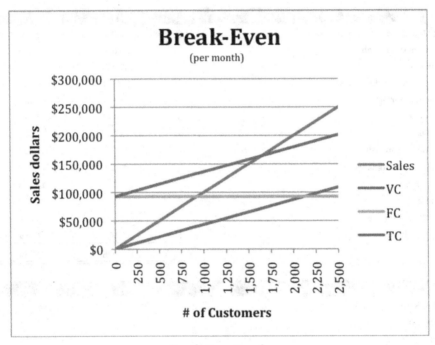

Break Even Graph

Supermarket Chain

Highlights of this Marketing Plan:
1. Good situational analysis using Porter's 5 Forces Model
2. Inclusion of several Perceptual Maps
3. Discussion on Brand Equity using the BVA Model

Executive Summary

An early entrant to the food retail market, Loblaw Companies Limited (Loblaw) has established itself as the largest food distributor and a leading provider of general merchandise products, drugstore and financial products and services in Canada. Though multiple operating banners, Loblaw has been committed to providing a one-stop shopping experience to its customers. It offers Canada's strongest control label program, including the unique President's Choice Financial Services with Insurance, Mobile phone and Points Loyalty program.

Loblaw has grown and occupies the leading position in the Supermarket space against other vendors such as Wal-Mart and Sobeys, where it caters to >30% of the market. In the last decade, this space has seen significant growth and competition, with most vendors venturing into Mergers & Acquisition (M&A) and organic growth, thus expanding their reach to underserved geographies at a national level. Extension and express outlets in the form of convenience stores have further spiked the competitive nature of this market, with eminent threat of substitute products and increasing competitor share within existing customer base. Refer to Section 2 for a detailed analysis of the Canadian Supermarket industry, using Michael Porter's 5-Forces model.

In this industry scenario, Loblaw has established a Marketing Mix where it continues to offer food products under different brands mapped to different target segments, but has expanded to offer other merchandise such as house-wares as well. In-house labels such as Presidents Choice have been extended to the highly successful Financial Products business, but the annual performance results from the last 4-5 years indicate failure in its core food product business, driven by the reduced focus and lack of speed with respect to embracing technological advances to improve operations such as supply chain and sourcing. Further analysis using Brand Asset Valuator for Brand Audit indicate similar findings – where the company fails to differentiate itself and display the energy of the brand to its consumers. See Section 3 for detailed SWOT Analysis on the Marketing Mix and Section 4 for Brand Audit and subsequent findings.

The Final section provides a consolidated view of all findings and provides a detailed time-bound action plan for reinforcement and revitalization of the Loblaw brand. In alignment with the Interbrand Brand Valuation method, it is proposed that Loblaw strengthen its value proposition to the customer through enhanced focus on its core food product offering, develop online channel for expansion of retail business, review & restructure its child brands for better alignment with the company's segment-oriented business and finally, use brand extension strategy to leverage its customer base across all different banners.

1.0 Analysis of Supermarket Industry in Canada

1.1 Industry Definition
Supermarkets are characterized as stores with over 15000 square feet of selling space, with very diverse products for sale, and located within a 15-minute drive from the clientele. The definition of a 'chain' used by Statistics Canada is an enterprise with more than 4 stores, with advantages related to wholesaling, warehousing, advertising and better use of advanced technology. The top 5 supermarket chains in Canada are Loblaws, Sobeys, Wal-Mart, Canada Safeway and Metro.

1.2 Industry Profile
Supermarkets represent about 15% of all Operating Revenue in the Retail sector in Canada. Considering all the pharmacies, personal care stores, convenience and specialty food outlets along with Supermarkets that are owned by the 'chains', the total Operating Revenue exceeds 35% of the sector, which is an indication of the large market for such institutions (see Exhibit A).

One of the most significant transformations is the shift to US-style superstore format, with improved store design, customer service and a trend to focus on specific ethnic niches. The ethnic focus is evident in Loblaw's recent acquisition of Canada's largest Asian food retailer T&T Supermarket Inc. for $225 million.

1.3 Forces impacting Profitability
While grocery profit margins are typically low, the superstore format generates higher customer traffic due to size, which also results in increased sales of higher-margin general merchandise goods. To understand the forces that impact profitability of stores in this sector, we utilize Michael Porter's 5-forces model.

Note: (+) indicates a positive force, (-) indicates a negative force and (o) indicates a neutral force that has both positive and negative impact on the dynamics of the industry with respect to Loblaw.

Bargaining Power of Suppliers (+)

- Supermarkets are large consumers and sellers of supplier products
- They can negotiate better prices based on large volumes that cannot be matched by smaller retailers
- Suppliers are threatened by the ability of large retailers to source from abroad at cheaper rates **(see Exhibit B)**
- Binding relationship with specific suppliers could constraint options for the large retailers, thus impacting margins.

Hence, Suppliers have low bargaining power and hence this is a positive factor for the supermarkets.

Threat of New Entrants (+)

- Canadian supermarket industry has been dominated by the top 5 chains, that cover more than 80% of the market
- Supermarket chains have strong efficiencies built around their operations, with larger bandwidth for aggressive promotions, target sales with one-stop shopping experience and advanced technology use such as RFID and self checkouts
- Need to raise large capital with substantial fixed costs in the difficult economy creates an entry barrier for new entrants

Hence, the threat of New Entrants in the industry is relatively small.

Bargaining Power of Customers (o)

- As consumer products have become more standardized and undifferentiated, switching costs for customers has reduced, thus yielding power to buyers
- By shopping in large numbers, buyers have provided supermarkets the opportunity to diversify into pharmacies, financial services and such other business lines that has increased revenue and profitability, with enhanced cross-sell options

Hence, though consumers could typically have high bargaining power, their contribution to store expansion and growth provides a neutral impact.

Threat of Substitute Products (-)

- The large presence of convenience stores in the neighborhood provides a ready option for consumers to opt for alternate products, when bulk buying is not in need
- Trade regulations such as NAFTA have ensured availability of alternate product options from low-cost origins such as Mexico. China also continues to be a large supplier of alternate low cost products

Hence, multiple options are available to consumers based on their preference for convenience, quantity, retail store efficiency and so on.

Competitive Rivalry within Industry (-)

- The Supermarkets and supporting retail dynamics have seen significant growth in the last decade, with greater store sizes, utilization of a range of formats, expansion into new geographies and improving supply chain efficiencies for lower operating costs and increasing margins, with minimal increase in product cost

- Expansion of international chains such as Wal-Mart marks a significant threat to domestic supermarket and smaller retail chains, challenging their selection of grocery/food/pharmacy products and other general merchandise

- While operating in a flat and mature market where growth is difficult (indicated by diversification into non-food products and an average industry growth rate of <6% Y-o-Y), consumers continue to be demanding and sophisticated

Thus, rivalry within the industry is highly competitive and current market leaders such as Loblaw need to refocus on price and value, while reinforcing the value-added elements of their customer proposition.

2.0 Market Position of Loblaws

Established over 50 years ago, Loblaw has grown to become an employer of over 139,000 associates with annual revenue of C$30 billion in 2008. It is one of the largest food distributors and supermarket chains in Canada with more than 1000 consumer touch-points, through a network of corporate, franchised and independent stores.

2.1 Marketing Mix – 4P Analysis

Target Market
- Specializes in low cost products using its size and efficiency of operations, along with product differentiation by encouraging President's Choice and other private labels
- Uses a wide variety of banners to position company products to different target segments

Primary Competitors
- Sobeys is the second largest food retailer in Canada with over 1300 supermarkets, also operating under a variety of banners with annual revenue of more than C$15 billion in 2008
- The presence of Wal-Mart with its highly efficient store operations, brand reputation/recognition and competitive pricing is a mighty challenger to Loblaws. This has been evident through Loblaw's desperate attempts in the last 3-4 years to integrate non-food merchandise in its product offering
- Metro is the third largest chain in Canada. With about 40,000 employees, its primary operations are in Quebec and Ontario

Marketing Mix

Product

- Provides a one-stop destination for Canadian customers for all their food and household needs

- Specialized innovative and low cost products sold through private labels and well known market brands

- Core business in the field of food and groceries which expanded into supermarkets in the 1980-1990s, which has further diversified into Banking and Credit card products under the private label of President's Choice

- Pioneer in providing enhanced customer service using technological advances such as price scanners for quick checkout

- Ethnic preferences such as Asian Food specialties are a focus area for the chain and recent M&A activity is geared towards this objective

- New chain of 'Real Canadian Super Stores (RCSS)' launched in 2000 with further rebranding in 2008. RCSS stores a variety of goods from food/groceries, to electronics, house-wares and clothing, as a competitive option to Wal-Mart.

Price

- Leveraging its large size, supply chain options, private labels and a variety of banners/store types, Loblaw has been able to price products based on target markets, geographies and consumer demographics

Place

- Using trade names such as Loblaws, Atlantic SaveEasy, Extra Foods, Fortinos, No Frills, Provigo, Your Independent Grocer and Zehr Markets, Loblaw is able to reach customers through stores from supermarket size to smaller local retail stores.

Promotion

- Loblaw utilizes a combination of TV and print campaigns with short-term in-store promotions as well as discount sales using its President's Choice Credit card line of business

- Emphasizing its use of local and fresh produce, Loblaw has effectively utilized TV ads to show the quality of its food products, that are sourced from local farms and orchards

2.2 Perceptual Map – Loblaws and its competitors

The key factors in the Supermarket industry with focus on retail sales of food and non-food items are as below:

1. Quality – Quality of product is paramount, especially when it comes to food and derived products.

2. Price – Ability to price the products effectively, considering sensitivities of each geography within the country, along with consideration for local provision stores that could cause a serious dent to supermarket margins

3. Convenience – The ability to buy groceries and other general merchandise from outlets

4. Efficiency – The ability to efficiently manage supply chain such that product inventory is available on store shelves with fast refill from warehouses

The following Perceptual maps define the positioning of Loblaw's chain of supermarkets with respect to Sobeys and Wal-Mart. The indicative sizing of the globe depicts the volume of business for each respective company.

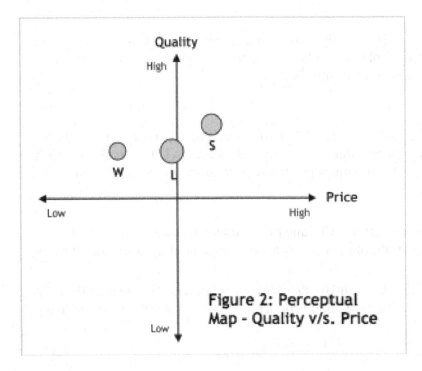

Figure 2: Perceptual Map - Quality v/s. Price

Perceptual Map (Quality/Price)

2.3 Analysis of Loblaws market strategy

Detailed analysis of Loblaw's Marketing Mix and its strategy vis-à-vis its competitors and general market dynamics is captured in the **SWOT analysis** below. The Opportunities section specifically lists the areas for improvement that should be pursued by Loblaw over the next few quarters.

Strengths

- Multiple store fronts catering to specific target markets under respective brands, thus using effective customer segmentation to address respective market needs which further roll up to Loblaw's market base

- Continued market leadership in the supermarket space, with 3% sales growth in H1-2009 thus proving its ability to attract and retain customers

- Popular in-house labels such as President's Choice which are leveraged well for its financial services business, thus providing cross-sell opportunities with its banking and supermarket/retail operations

Weaknesses

- 4 continuous years of poor financial growth from 2004 to H1-2008 indicated the company's inability to scale its operations in terms of efficiency and optimization

- Concentration on non-food products during the above timeframe reduced the focus on food products which is being revived only in the last 3-4 quarters

- Continuous organic and inorganic growth has meant that little critical evaluation has been done for store-banners that are not performing as expected; with ongoing overhead expense of payroll and administration

Opportunities

- Expand services in the online retail space. Loblaws currently does not provide customers the ability to check for product availability in stores or to place online orders for future delivery

- Utilize enhanced technology options to improve supply chain efficiencies, source from wider and cheaper suppliers in the local geography and review the breadth of product variety offered in its supermarkets to compete with stalwarts such as Wal-Mart

- Perform detailed evaluation of its product offerings at local retail level in addition to its supermarket business, to improve responsiveness and competitive position against local competitors or extensions of its national competitors (such as Sobeys).

Threats
- New M&A activity at national level by Sobeys and Metro along with expansion of Wal-Mart is a huge threat to Loblaw's core supermarket business
- Inability to differentiate the value of its product offerings apart from the popular private labels impacts customer loyalty and provides little reason to not explore competitor stores for better offers; thus reducing the competition to a pricing war

3.0 Evaluation of Brand Equity for Loblaws

Brand Equity is the added value endowed on products and services, which is reflected in:
- The way consumers think, feel and act with respect to the brand, as well as
- In the prices, market share and profitability that the brand commands for the firm.

Brand Audit is an important process that can be utilized to evaluating such brand equity, using a combination of qualitative and quantitative research.

3.1 Valuation of Brand Equity

A typical Brand Audit is conducted using the following 3 steps:

1. Inventory of all elements associated with the band – name, logo, brand positioning, marketing activities such as advertising and promotion

2. Consumer Perceptions – perception of the consumers regarding the brand's logo, it's positioning statement and change in marketing strategy based on inputs from insight gathered from field associates and consumers

3. Quantitative Tools – detailed study of consumer perception and likes-dislikes about each element identified in the inventory (step 1)

Considering the cost and turnaround time associated with a detailed Customer survey, the Brand Audit for Loblaw for this report has been conducted using:

- Facts known about the brand through its marketing mix
- Branding strategy adopted by the company through its different segment-focused banners
- Sales and growth performance results indicated by its financial performance over the last few years

The Brand Asset Valuator (BAV) tool created by Young and Rubicam provides comparative measures for brand equity that can be used to identify the current strength of the brand and a possible list of action items that can be used to improve the weak factors, as derived from this model. The five key components defined by BAV are:

1. Differentiation – measures the degree to which a brand is viewed differently from competitors

2. Energy – measures the brand's sense of momentum

3. Relevance – measures the brand's appeal to a breadth of customer needs

4. Esteem – measure of the brand's respect and regard to the customers

5. Knowledge – measure of the familiarity and intimacy of the brand with its customer base

The following table captures elements of the Loblaws brand, perception of the respective element and relevance to one or more parameters from the BAV tool. The current Brand status of Loblaw has accordingly been derived.

Element	Message and Perception	Impact on BAV Parameters
Name and Logo	- Loblaw's name and logo has been consistent through the decades of its presence - Logos adopted by Loblaw's banners such as President's Choice, Dominion and Independent have great similarity to the parent logo in terms of font and colour combination - They have considerable recall and recognition value which is apparent through the consistent leadership position that Loblaws has enjoyed through the decades	Esteem – High Knowledge - High
Brand Positioning	- Loblaw claims to be a 'one-stop' destination for meeting food and household needs - Its in-house labels such as *President's Choice (Financial)*, *no name* (Food) and *Joe Fresh* (Clothing) have their unique positioning and are considered to be largely successful in food and non-food products - Competitors such as Sobeys have similar in-house labels which are widely popular in the retail space	Differentiation – Medium Relevance – High Esteem - High Knowledge – High
Product portfolio	- Loblaw's Corporate profile states that it is the 'largest' food distributor and a 'leading' provider of non-food products such as general merchandise and financial services - Such product portfolio is synonymous with other large retailers in the Canadian retail space, such as Wal-Mart and Sobeys	Differentiation – Low
Marketing Strategy	- Considering the market's preference for 'Green' environment-friendly products and need for 'Organic' food options, Loblaw introduced GREEN reusable shopping bags in 2007. - Similarly, organic food products and an environment-friendly superstore have emphasized the company's commitment to such initiatives - Most supermarket chains followed this lead and have introduced green products such as shopping bags which has neutralized the long-term impact for Loblaw	Differentiation – Low Relevance – High Esteem – High
Growth rates	- Creating a store with near-equal focus on food and other merchandise has diluted the claim of Loblaw being 'THE'	Differentiation – Low

Analysis of Loblaws branding using BAV

From the above analysis, the current Brand position of Loblaw is derived as: Differentiation – Low, Energy – Low, Relevance – High, Esteem – High, Knowledge – High

Using the BAV model, this evaluation positions Loblaw in the 'Declining' class of brands.

3.2 Key Issues and Action Items

Building further on the evaluation done in the previous section, the key parameters that need to be revived to move the Loblaw brand from a 'Declining' to a 'Leadership' status are: Differentiation and Energy.

Effective Brand management requires a 2-dimensional review of the current brand value and the marketing activities associated with it, as described below --

1. **Brand Reinforcement:** Key action items under this category include -

    *   Reverse downward trend in brand value by focusing on the core benefits that the brand has been known for. In case of Loblaw, this would be Quality of Food products

    *   Reinforce superior position of the brand by associating its food products with international certification norms such as those offered by Global Trust Certification for agricultural and seafood based products

2. **Brand Revitalization:** Key action items under this category include –

    *   The low energy element of the brand needs to be revitalized by understanding changing needs and preferences of customers and disassociating with the negative perception of slow change

    *   Revive old positioning of being a leading technology adopter and reinvent itself by offering additional sales channels in addition to the traditional store-counter method used for decades

The detailed action items with timelines have been rolled up into Short and Long term strategies for Loblaw, as described in the next section.

4.0 Strategic Recommendations

Following is the consolidated list of Opportunities and Key improvement area, identified from the SWOT analysis and Brand Audit for Loblaw, with due consideration to the applicable forces in the Supermarket and food retail industry:

*   Reverse downward trend in brand value by focusing on the core benefits that the brand has been known for. In case of Loblaw, this would be Quality of Food products.

*   Revive old positioning of being a leading technology adopter and reinvent by offering additional sales channels such as the Internet

*   Expand services in the online retail space

*   Utilize enhanced technology options to improve supply chain efficiencies

- Reinforce superior position of the brand by associating its food products with international certification norms
- Understand changing needs and preferences of customers and disassociate with the negative perception of slow change

Additionally, review of the existing brands to measure their success and utility to the Loblaw portfolio and counter-actions for threat of substitute products and initiatives undertaken by competitors are equally important to the future marketing strategy for the company.

The following sections capture key changes to the Marketing Strategy for Loblaw, to have a bottom-line impact to its Brand Value and ensure increase in growth and retention of its Leadership position in the Canadian market. These have been aligned with the Interbrand Brand Valuation Method.

4.1 Short-Term Strategy

The following Action Items are suggested for the next 2 Quarters (3-6 months)

Understand and Address Demand Drivers:

1. <u>Re-focus on its core offering of being a leader in food product retail</u> – Re-create the differentiating factor of being the best retailer in the Canadian food market. This could be done by emphasizing on the largest variety of locally and internationally produced food varieties. Considering that Canadian customers place emphasis on local produce, Loblaw should ensure accurate placement of such products in their stores to attract the right customer segment. Filing for international quality certifications on the food products will further create elite positioning of this store vis-à-vis its domestic and international competition.

Potential Impact: Food products return as the core product offering from Loblaw and products for each target segment develop a unique elite position against other convenience and supermarket chain stores.

Risk: Potential loss of business in general merchandise and household needs. This can be effectively mitigated by increase in food product sales and creating a separate niche for Loblaw brand as against Wal-Mart and Sobeys.

2. <u>Enhanced use of technology</u> – Develop online website to provide facility to check for product availability through the web or in a particular store, and support web orders with online payment and options for products to be shipped or picked up from a local store.

Potential Impact: Creation of new customer base of online buyers, especially the working class of people who could do groceries 24*7, from the comfort of their home.

Risk: There could be a reduction on sales of associated products that are dependent on other core quality product lines, but this could be mitigated by providing insight into such products on the website itself.

4.2 Long-Term Strategy

The following Action Items are suggested on a long term basis for the next 1-3 Years --

Perform Competitive Benchmarking:

1. <u>Assess and restructure brand portfolio</u> - Evaluate performance of all individual brands in the Loblaw portfolio to measure their revenue and profitability trends, along with their inherent role in the company's value proposition. With each brand supposed to be focused on an identified market segment, their current operations should be mapped to identify overlaps and conflicting positioning to the customer. The brands should accordingly be restructured to align with existing and new market segments, with focused view on addressing competitive advances at each level and utilizing economies of scale wherever possible.

Potential Impact: Possibility of sunk costs and reinvestment into existing and new brand values. Such short term expenses will provide benefit on a long term basis by better margins and reduced loss of customers' value share.

Risk: Difficult to balance reinvestments and business restructuring aspects, in compliance with social norms and government regulations; this will have to be mitigated on a case-by-case basis.

Develop Brand Strength:

2. <u>Develop Stronger Brand line</u> – Improve Brand awareness by creating stronger association of child brands with the parent Loblaw brand. This could be done by aligning all logos closer to the parent logo and / or adding a supporting tag line such as "<name of brand> – a Loblaw enterprise". Such association can be used for brand extension by creating Loyalty programs and offering volume discounts across different banners.

Potential Impact: Better recognition and esteem associated with the brand and knowledge of Loblaw's association becoming a commonly known fact, rather than being limited to the urban elite who are aware of brand associations.

Risk: Unique value associated with child brands may get diluted to an extent, but this can be prevented by continuing the value and service provided by these brands, while indicating added financial stability and historical reputation associated with the parent company.

Conclusion, Appendix and Reference Sections are removed intentionally.

Transportation Service

Highlights of this Marketing Plan:
1. A short-and-concise piece that tells the story well
2. Good use of bullet points to highlight key ideas
3. Break-even analysis

Executive Summary

DrinkBuddy Taxi Service (DTS) is a new kind of transportation company. Through our partnerships with the Boston Red Sox, Sam Adams Brewery, local and state law enforcement, our sound business practices, and unwavering ethical values, we aim to be THE transportation company of choice for young working adults and college students in and around Metro West Boston. Unlike traditional taxi services and mass transportation we offer people who have consumed one too many drinks the option of having a sober diver pick them up and drive them home in their own vehicle while a second employee follows them to pick up our driver once the patron and their vehicle are at their destination safely. Like our motto says, "Why take the risk when we can drive? Call us today, and you can rest assured that both you and your vehicle will arrive home safely. We Guarantee it."

A transportation company that caters to both the adult driver and their vehicle is a rarity in the Boston area. This provides DTS with an opportunity to enter a market with little known competition and a strong demand for service. DTS will achieve significant market penetration and steady sustainable growth as outlined in our marketing and business plan. Through our direct to the consumer approach, we will maintain a close relationship with our customers and continue to adapt to their needs as we grow.

DrinkBuddy Taxi Service will be recognized as number choice for both you and your vehicle to arrive home safely in the transportation industry. We will offer our customers an effective and safe transportation service within the metro west Boston areas while catering to market segments that can benefit from our services. This will provide for sound return on investment and sustainable growth.

Product or Service Description

The product/service that DrinkBuddy Taxi Service (DTS) is bringing to market is a designated driver service that will operate similar to a taxi services. This service will offer people who have consumed one too many drinks the option of having a sober diver pick them up and drive them home in their own vehicle while a second employee follows them to pick up our driver once the patron and their vehicle are at their destination safely. This service will operate in the greater Boston and surrounding suburban communities and will book reservations through our toll free number (888-we-drive), text messaging, and web reservation.

We will employ a variety of employees that can operate vehicles ranging from your run of the mill family sedan all the way to commercial vehicles requiring a CDL license to operate. Furthermore, all of our drivers will be required to obtain a hackney license or medallion, take and pass the AAA driver improvement program, have a clean driving record, be at least 25 years old with 7 years driving experience, and submit to random drug and alcohol testing.

SWOT Analysis

Strengths:
- Minimal competition in our geographic location for this service
- The use of multi licensed drivers who can operate a wide range of vehicles
- Well-trained employees
- Confidentiality. We will not release client information without a court order requesting us to do so
- 24-hour service
- Provides a safe alternative to driving drunk
- Low startup costs

Weaknesses:
- A lack of partnerships while entering the marketplace
- Resistances of car owner to letting a stranger drive their car home
- A lack of awareness for the service we provide
- Lack of brand name recognition due to startup nature of the business

Opportunities:
- The ability to collaborate with local area bars, restaurants, and nightclubs
- Increased police presence and checkpoints discouraging drunk driving
- Steady future demand for this service
- Partnership with local college and professional sport venues

Threats:
- Local government regulation of industry
- Future competition
- Economic depression
- Consumer resistance to service

Market Summary

DrinkBuddy Taxi Service is well informed about the potential cliental Boston, Ma and its surrounding suburbs have to offer. This information will be utilized to tailor our needs to our cliental and better understand what our clients are looking for and how we can go about providing this for them.

Target Markets

- Young Professionals
- College Students
- Blue Collar Workers
- Nigh Life
- Sports Fans

Market Demographics

The profile of the typical DrinkBuddy Taxi Service customer consists of the following geographic, demographic, and behavioral factors.

Geographic

- DrinkBuddy Taxi Service is targeting Middlesex County in Massachusetts
- Total population for this area consists of approximately 1,482,478 permanent residents as of 2008, not including transient college students

Demographics

- There is a 49% to 51% ratio of males to females in this demographic
- Ages 18-35
- 43.6% of customers over 25 have a bachelor degree or higher
- Median household income of $78,040

Behavior Factors

- Users enjoy an active nightlife as a means to unwind after a stressful day at work
- Users spend money on overnight parking and a taxi services after drinking too much during a night out

- Users have an active social life that involves going to sports events, clubs, or other social events where alcohol tends to be served

Market Needs

DrinkBuddy Taxi Service is providing the nightlife and sport fan community in Middlesex County with a safe and secure service to transport themselves and their vehicle home after a night out on the town. We seek to fulfill the following needs of our consumers:

- **Safe Travel**. Provide a cost effective means to transport both individual and their vehicle home safely
- **Worry free pickups.** Simply give us a call, text, or schedule online ahead of time and a pair of our drivers will be there to transport the person and their vehicle home safely

Market Trends

DrinkBuddy Taxi Service will distinguish itself from the competition by marketing a service that has very little core competition. Previously our consumers would need to leave their cars over night and find an alternate way home or risk driving and suffering the consequences of a penalty if caught. Companion Diving Service will allow our customers to fully enjoy themselves without having to worry about how they will not only get themselves home in a safe and affordable manner but also their vehicle.

Market Growth

With the penalties for first time arrest becoming increasingly more costly to consumers in Middlesex County our market is ripe for growth. A first time offense in MA can result in "Up to 30 Months in jail, A fine from $500 to $5,000, A $250 Assessment, $50 towards the DUI Victim Trust Fund, A license suspension of 1 Year, and completion of a court assigned treatment program". We believe that our market will continue to grow proportionately with consumers reaching the age of 21.

Critical Issues

- Establish DrinkBuddy Taxi Service as the transportation alternative in Middlesex County
- Pursue continued sustainable growth ensuring our expenses do not exceed our revenue base
- Continually strive to improve customer satisfaction, ensuring that we exceed our competition in all areas. We will never comprise customer satisfaction in order to grow our market share

Marketing Strategy

DrinkBuddy Taxi Service's marketing strategy is to focus on print advertisements at high visibility locations our customers frequent. Through partnerships with the Boston Red Sox, Sam Adams Brewery, local and state law enforcement, and other local establishments and hotspots, we will be able to reach all of the segments within the market.

Marketing Objectives

- Develop a loyal customer base
- Establish and maintain positive sustainable growth
- Listen to customers' needs and desires to enable us to plan future vehicle purchase so that they are aligned with consumer wants

Marketing Mix

DrinkBuddy Taxi Services' marketing mix is comprised of the following strategies for pricing, distribution, advertising and promotion, and customer service.

- **Pricing:** Our pricing is designed to be more affordable than simply taking a taxi service home. We guarantee our customers that we will provide transportation home for $4.00 less than what a taxi fare would costs (including return trip the following day to pick up vehicle). Our pricing structure is based on the distance required to deliver a customer and his or her vehicle home safely.

- **Distribution:** DrinkBuddy Taxi Services' will use a direct to consumer distribution model. Customers will schedule pickups via our online scheduling system (on the company web site), through text messages to our dispatching center, or via phone calls to out dispatchers.

- **Advertising and Promotion:** We will utilize several differ types of media for advertising and promotion. Radio advertisements slotted at the 5-7pm timeframe on popular sports radio and top 40 stations will be utilized along with commercials during local broadcasts of sporting events. Through our partnership with local pubs and clubs, we will offer customers five free rides as part of our initial entry into the market. Print advertising will be posted in restrooms at local drinking establishments and along the outside of Fenway Park. In addition to traditional advertising means, our partnership with local and state law enforcement has resulted in numbers stories on our business in the local newspapers and on local news stations.

- **Customer Service:** We will strive to offer our customers the best transportation experience possible. Meeting and exceeding that of our competition.

Financials

Break-Even Analysis:

DTS anticipates and average selling price per ride for our service at $15.00. This includes direct costs of $2.00 per trip for fuel, $1.00 per trip for vehicle upkeep, and $3.00 towards the wage and benefits of the driver per trip, these are our direct costs. This results in a Contribution Margin (CM) of $9.00 per trip. The CM covers fixed costs and OH expenses (indirect costs) such as the monthly lease payment, hackney license fee, marketing, and insurance amounts. Our monthly lease payment for the dispatch center is $950.00 and our monthly insurance for the company is $935.00. This gives us fixed costs per month of $1885.00. In order for our service to break even (BE) each month, we will need to make 210 trips per month or 53 per week.

- CM= $15.00-$6.00 (direct costs) = $9.00
- FC/CM=$1,885.00/$9.00= 210
- BE=210 trips per month, 53 trips per week, 8 trips per day
- Monthly Units to Break-Even: 210
- Monthly Sales to Break-Even: $3,150
- Average Per Unit Revenue: $15.00
- Average Per-Unit Variable Costs: $6.00
- Estimated Monthly Fixed: $6.00
- Estimated Monthly Fixed Costs: $1,885

Sales Forecast:

DTS has projected its sales figures on a conservative basis for fiscal years 2010, 2011, and 2012. This budget will allow for steady growth throughout our first three years as we establish ourselves as the leader in our market.

Sales	2010	Sales Forecast $$ 2011	2011
Young Professionals	$100,000	$145,000	$174,000
Blue Collar Workers	$60,000	$70,000	$89,000
College Students	$20,000	$25,000	$37,000
Total Sales	$180,000	$240,000	$300,000
Direct Cost of Sales			
Young Professionals	$46,669	$67,669	$81,200
Blue Collar Workers	$28,000	$32,669	$41,531
College Students	$9,331	$11,669	$17,269
Subtotal Cost of Sales	$84,000	$112,007	$140,000
Sales Per Year	2010	Sales Forecast Units 2011	2011
Young Professionals	6,667	9,667	11,600
Blue Collar Workers	4,000	4,667	5,933
College Students	1,333	1,667	2,467
Total Sales	12,000	16,001	20,000
Sales Per week			
Young Professionals	128	186	223
Blue Collar Workers	77	90	114
College Students	26	32	47
Sales Per Week	231	308	385

Sales Forecasts (Revenue and Unit)

Marketing Expense Budget:

Our marketing expense budget is based off the current market prices for air-time on WEEI 850am Boston, MA's premier sports radio station per our conversation with John Capuano, WEEI director of sales on June 11, 2010.

- 30-second spot during Red Sox game broadcast $1500-2500.
- 30-second spot during morning or evening commuting hours $800.

The majority of our revenues in the first three years of operation will be directed towards our marketing campaign. This will allow us to distinguish ourselves from out competition and establish ourselves as "the" transportation service in Metro west Boston. After FY 2012, we anticipate annual marketing costs reducing annually until they represent 10% of total sales.

Marketing Expense Budget	2010	2011	2012
Web Site	$18,775	$6,500	$$7,000
Radio Spots	$50,000	$67,000	$80,000
Printed Material	$2,500	$5,000	$3,000
Free Ride Promotion	$7,500	$0.00	$0.00
Total	$78,775	$79,000	$90,000
Percent of Sales	43.76%	32.9%	30.0%
Contribution Margin	$143,000	$189,000	$237,000
CM/Sales	79.44%	78.75%	79.00%

Marketing Budget

Conclusion:

DrinkBuddy Taxi Service is fulfilling an unmet market needs in the transportation sector due to lack of similar service in town. Annual sales revenue is estimated to be $180K, $240K, and $300K respectively for the first three years of operation, with a break-even requirement of 210 trips per month. The majority of the marketing expense will be allocated to web site promotion and radio advertisement. The management believes that this marketing plan is an operationally feasible and financially attractive one.

Chapter 5 –
Marketing Plan Example –
Consumer Products

Smartphone

Highlights of this Marketing Plan:
1. Good SWOT analysis
2. "Six Box" method is used
3. Detailed Brand Audit discussion

1.0   Executive Summary

i-mate™, has been selling and marketing Microsoft® Windows Mobile® technology since 2001. The current market operates in perfect competition, and i-mate™ is in declining phase as it focuses on cost containment and a 'back to basics' approach. It has found the US market tough due to patent regulations, but sees opportunity in emerging markets Russia and India. It also considers consolidation of entrenched Australasian and Middle Eastern markets.

i-mate™ has low supplier power due to the competitive nature of the industry, and low buyer power as it does not own the supplier and distributors in the supply chain. There are eight leading competitors on the Microsoft sight, including an ex-supplier who has leading market intelligence and intellectual property due to its past relationship with i-mate™. It is easy to enter and exit the industry market.

i-mate™ has reduced a number of staff, is considering withdrawal from the US market and is projecting new product introduction in 2010. There have been a number of issues with two of its new suppliers which have resulted in late deliveries and product specification not matching consumer expectations which although have been resolved through Quality

Assurance processes and responsibilities in the service level agreements, have thwarted growth in some regions. In addition, the recent withdrawal from the AIM stock market has created consumer unease in viability.

Latest international strategies have been to withdraw from the US, purchase a smartphone manufacturer and software development house in China and to focus on emerging and already entrenched markets, all of which are recommended. Re-launching the brand is not recommended as there is brand equity in the current brand which should be leveraged in difficult market conditions.

The positioning of the product shows a desired belief that i-mate™ products are state-of-the art and supply chain and customer touch points are all reliable providing total customer satisfaction. The target market in each of the regions is the technologically and communicatively savvy 'Y Generation'. There are key features that i-mate™ should market which are: portability and durability (weight, size, stamina and robustness), sound and picture quality, complementary products such as hands free, speed and looks. Short-term branding should focus on these features whereas long-term branding strategies should focus on state-of-the-art technology to drive sales.

Recent brand issues relate to the delisting on the stock market and the US withdrawal. Approaches dedicated to honest and transparent communication on these issues and proposed solutions are recommended.

Lastly, an overview of the marketing mix; Product, Price, Place and Promotion indicated the focus of the marketing strategy in the year ahead.

2.0   Situational Analysis

i-mate™ is a global smartphone supplier, marketing and distributing direct to consumers and with support of service centres across distribution markets. The business operates in a single business segment, being hardware. As opposed to a monopoly or oligopoly, i-mate™ operates in perfect competition, with many firms competing for overall low market share. All offer similar products and have the ability to enter and exit the market freely. Information is readily accessible to all participants in the vertical supply chain.

As a supplier of Microsoft® Windows Mobile® technology operating since 2001, i-mate™ is in a declining phase, whereby it has a large decrease in sales and is now consolidating and focusing on cost reductions. i-mate™ is focusing on product development and quick release to be first to market in a highly competitive industry of rapid change and technological advances. i-mate™ is building demand through global reach in various continents.

2.0.1 Market Summary

The telecommunications industry has experienced a rapid decline in sales, particularly in corporate volumes. Despite this, the industry continues to rapidly change with new research and development and subsequent releases of products new to market. Microsoft competes against Apple to provide leading edge mobile technology.

Competition has become fiercer with new OEM companies entering the market. Due to the downturn in the economy sales have declined markedly. However, there are emerging markets in India and Russia that provide potential for growth.

2.0.2   Five Forces Analysis

Porter's (1979) Five Forces Analysis provides an overview of competitive power for i-mate™.

Supplier Power

Supplier products are critical for i-mate™ to proceed in business. Losing HTC has resulted in costly litigation issues. Changing the supplier to two suppliers; Taiwan's Inventec and China's TechFaith, has resulted in logistic and supply chain management issues through poor quality control, and subsequent delays in product release and sales. Currently i-mate is totally dependant on these suppliers. The cost of changing suppliers again would mean any costs associated with setting up TechFaith and Inventec would be sunk costs. Similarly, the procurement agreement may have a termination clause that does not allow for change.

Buyer Power

As i-mate™ is a global business, buyer power can vary depending on its dominance and brand equity in each of the foreign markets. However, there are a number of competitors like i-mate™ in the global market, so buyers can drive the price of units down. i-mate™ targets business enterprise and so large corporations using i-mate™ products and services can further drive down costs through procurement agreements.

Competitive Rivalry

There are a number of competitor suppliers in the market , with 50 device manufacturers and 160 mobile operators in 55 countries designing or offering Windows Mobile devices. i-mate™ has the license to Microsoft® Windows Mobile® technology to support PC integration. However, there are a number of competitor suppliers in smartphone products in the market, as listed below:

a.   HP
b.   HTC
c.   Motorolla
d.   Palm
e.   Pantech
f.   Psion Teklogix
g.   Samsung
h.   Verizon

Threat of Substitution

Due to the array of competitive products in the market, customers will always compare substitute products. Substitution is easy, cheap and viable for consumers, weakening power. Microsoft is supporting many developers to develop and distribute Microsoft technology with online end-to-end advice.

Threat of New Entry
HTC's recent move from ODM to smartphone marketer and supplier, exemplifies the easy entry competitors have in the market. i-mate™ must now work on litigation against HTC who has intellectual property on i-mate™ products, and competitor intelligence to position themselves strongly against i-mate™ in the market. There is a high risk that TechFaith and Inventec could also do the same, resulting in a weak position for i-mate™.

Complementary Products
i-mate™ also offers i-mate Go to provide touch screen technology, English to Japanese and Chinese conversion, security options and customization to complement the basic smartphone technology.

2.0.3 Target Markets
i-mate™ segments are geographical, operating in the following areas, Middle East, Australasia, Africa, Italy, UK, Rest of Europe, North America and Asia. It has focused on corporate sales as the target market. i-mate™ is now focusing on established markets in the Middle East and Australasia, as well as the new emerging markets in Russia and India where there is significant opportunity.

2.0.4 Factors that Influence Purchasing Decisions

1. Income of Buyers-products are sourced for business purposes and so businesses usually purchase for employees

2. Price of Product-product pricing needs to be competitive in a competitive market

3. Brand Quality-this is the most critical factor for consumers as they must rely on the technology to conduct business

4. Price of related goods-goods such as handsets must also be competitive

5. Seasonal Factors-Corporate consumers require the state-of-the art technology to improve business offering so can upgrade regularly

2.0.5 Price Discrimination
i-mate™ does not offer price discrimination as it does not have power in the market.

2.0.6 i-mate™ SWOT Analysis

Strengths

1. i-mate™ has six devices in the market and all are in the top of their class in terms of speed, output video quality and probably the best non-failure rate of any set of devices. The high-end devices have been well received by customers and industry specialists alike.

2. Introducing new products in 2010 and the early market response from established customers has been very encouraging.

3. In-house customer support that requires less resource due to new technology.

4. Markets in Middle East and Australasia are well established.

Weaknesses

1. Slow delivery of devices, and non-availability of devices in some regions, particularly for legacy products, resulting in lost momentum in several markets which is taking a while to re-establish.

2. i-mate™ has shed its software development team, its centralized Quality Assurance team (QA responsibility rests with suppliers), and many of the senior management team to reduce labour costs. This could result in less innovation.

3. Product quality issues from new suppliers that should now be resolved but requires monitoring.

4. Complications in target market specification requirements.

5. Delayed consumer acceptance of some of the new product ranges.

Opportunities

1. The presence of emerging markets and opportunity in Russia and India.

2. Smaller company through restructure has meant a stronger focus on core basic business rather than business acquisition and research and development costs.

3. Suppliers based in Taiwan and China that provides ideal geographical positioning to distribute into emerging markets.

Threats

1. Technology companies operating within the USA market need to deal with the USA patent system/IP infringements.

2. High-end complementary product sales such as handsets are declining in recent global downturn.

3.0 International Marketing Strategy

i-mate™ intends to implement the following strategy in global operations:

1. Closing the US Office

    This is a good strategy in the short term as growth has been stifled by regulatory patent requirements. Closing down the US office also results in labour cost savings. As Microsoft is based in the US, there is a great deal of competitors focusing on this market and so i-mate™ should consider growth potential in the market gaps. Exiting the US market altogether means that consumers will move to other brands. However, as the i-mate™ office has already shed head count and received negative press, it is best to enter the market again when market conditions are more favourable in the political and economic macro-environment.

2. Re-launch the company

    i-mate™ has had poor press based on its US operations and has also received a very poor annual report resulting in being de-listed on the AIM stock exchange. When in a global and competitive market where information is easy to obtain and share, the result has been a negative impact to its reputation. Therefore, re-launching the company to reflect the new international strategy and product offerings in 2010 initially sounds advisable. However, i-mate™ wants to improve sales in markets where it already has a strong foothold. To lose brand equity in these markets would be like starting again as a new entrant in the market. Similarly, new markets in Russia and India do not know the brand yet and so if launching in those regions under i-mate™, it should still do well. I would therefore recommend against re-launching the brand but if i-mate™ was to re-enter the US market, it should do this under another brand name exclusive to that market/ region.

3. Purchase a smartphone manufacturer and software development house in China

    Technologically i-mate™ has demonstrated poor performance recently through QA issues and target market specifications. Using suppliers raises risk as i-mate™ are not owning their intellectual property and have little control of supplier outputs, particularly if they are one of many companies the suppliers provide for. Moving into both hardware and software development provides a comprehensive supply chain to improve distribution and cost efficiencies. China is also in a geographically convenient position to distribute to both emerging markets and to Australasia which also provides cost savings in production and distribution.

4. Focus on established and emerging markets

   There are approximately 80 million adults in Russia and India is the second most populous country in the world. With the population, opportunities emerge in these markets for new entry suppliers of smartphone technology. i-mate™ should take early entry advantage in these markets ahead of competition. The telecommunications industry can have late entry advantage for companies who provide leading-edge technology. However, the recent technology from smartphone and i-phone only show tweaks to current product offerings. i-mate™ should also consolidate market share and sales in current established markets in Australasia and the Middle East. In order to support growth in software development and entry into emerging markets, i-mate™ needs to remain profitable in these regions.

4.0   Brand Audit
A brand audit helps understand the sources of brand equity and how they affect outcomes.

4.0.1 Inventory
Positioning Statement: i-mate™, is one of the world's leading experts in the design, development and customization of Microsoft® Windows Mobile® powered mobile devices. i-mate™ provides both product and service to corporates and individuals.

Packaging: an 'out of box' experience with consumers automatically configuring devices as soon as the SIM card is inserted.

Advertising: Online through i-mate™ site and also on Microsoft's site.

Distribution: through two suppliers in Asia, distribution globally.

4.0.2 Consumer Perceptions
IT industry reporters give favourable reviews on the i-mate™ 810F (displayed on company website). For example," "Brain meets brawn, the 810-F is the tough guy of the smartphone world". - T3 Magazine.

   CEO, Jim Morrison, states, "All are in the top of their class in terms of speed, output video quality and probably the best non-failure rate of any set of devices. The high-end Ultimate devices in particular have been well received by customers and industry specialists alike." (2008)

4.0.3 Quantitative Tools

Data on consumer preference in phone features are collected on website.

In summary, there are three steps to building a brand; defining the positioning and position why the brand is better than competitors, identify the target audience and construct the brand image. Its online site demonstrates that i-mate™ has achieved in the first two areas but could improve in the last. However, the annual report insinuates that i-mate™ could also improve on working with consumers to ensure specifications and product fit improve.

4.0.4 Short Term and Long Term Branding Strategies

There are three steps to building a brand; define the brand positioning, identify the target audience and construct a brand image. Some of the pitfalls that occur in this are failing to clearly establish a position or changing position too frequently, adding line extensions that dilute the positioning or introducing extensions that don't fit with the brand. In order to improve market share, i-mate™ should firstly define the brand position. This is done below firstly through the 'Convince-that-because' and then the 'Six Box' method.

4.0.5 Brand Position

1. 'Convince-that-because' Method

   Convince: Corporate and business people

   That: i-mate™ is one of the world's leading experts in the design, development and customization of Microsoft® Windows Mobile® powered mobile devices

   Because: i-mate™ phones are state-of-the art in Microsoft® Windows Mobile® powered mobile devices for design and features.

2. 'Six Box' Method

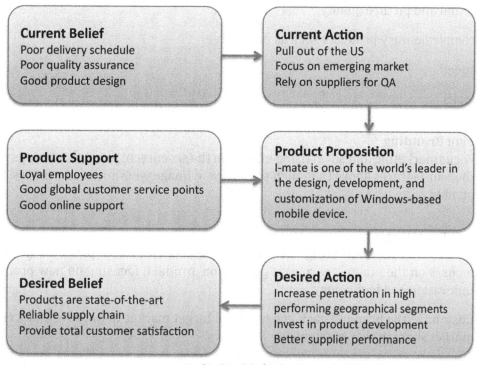

Six Box Method

4.0.6 Target Audience

The target audience for i-mate™ is business professionals in each region it serves, predominantly targeting the younger 'Y' generation and younger (born after 1980). This is because this generation is reported to be communication savvy in comparison to older generations. Business professionals are the most likely to need the Microsoft® Windows Mobile® smartphone technology due to mobility requirements and the need to have an 'office' at their fingertips. The overwhelming majority of Y generation owns a computer, a cell phone and a MP3 player and use technology as a social medium.

4.0.7 Brand Image

Consumers purchase products to fulfill needs, increase status, solve problems, enhance style or increase inner wellbeing. i-mate™ smartphones need to also serve the core function of communication, the formal function of doing so using mobile technology, and the augmented function of providing multiple features to achieve this communication.

i-mate™ has to appeal to the target audience and therefore needs to focus on features that will appeal to a consumer who uses their phone with great frequency and also uses their phone for social interaction as opposed to basic communication alone. With that in mind, i-mate™ needs to focus on:

1. portability and durability (weight, size, stamina and robustness)

2. sound and picture quality

3. complementary products such as hands free

4. speed

5. looks

Short-Term Branding
1. Focus marketing and advertising efforts on the six current product offerings and the four features above that align to the brand image we want in consumers' top of mind.

Long-Term Branding
1. Ensure that the marketing surrounding the launch of new products in 2010 focuses on the i-mate™ as a 'next generation' product, focusing on new product innovation and technology.

2. Customize the brand to each geographical target market to improve chances of market share in that segment.

3. Consider specialized target markets for the features. For example, durability may appeal to those in more robust trades instead of commercial professions.

5.0   Public Relations

There are a number of public relations tools available to i-mate™; press kits, speeches, seminars, annual reports, charitable donations, publications, community relations, lobbying, identity media and a company magazine (Kotler and Keller, 2009). In order to minimize the negative public reaction to the recent stock delisting from AIM as well as product delays, the following steps are recommended:

1. Provide an honest and transparent reason for the recent stock delisting and product delays in the annual report. Own up to failings but also provide solutions to these problems. Also signal to the market what i-mate™ expects their position to be in one year's time, so that consumers can see confidence returning.

2. Ensure all employees understand what has happened and why and also what i-mate™ is doing to remedy public faith so that they can also respond accurately when asked by consumers (perhaps through the intranet or cascaded through staff briefings).

3. Provide monthly press statements outlining company progress and improvements so that consumers see sustained, positive change. For example, sales above forecast, new contracts won and new product releases.

4. Advertise positive quotes from industry specialists and credible consumers who are very satisfied with the product and endorse its features and benefits.

5. Be seen as an industry leader through strategic placement of media articles on and in the industry.

6.0   Marketing Mix

Outlined in this section is the marketing mix for i-mate™.

6.0.1   Product

i-mate™ currently offer the following six products (descriptions below courtesy of Microsoft):

i-mate Ultimate 9502

The Ultimate 9502 offers a wide-range of mobile functionality, including built-in GPS; slide-out QWERTY keyboard; 2.8-inch VGA touch screen; Windows Mobile software; and i-Q services for remote device management.

i-mate Ultimate 8502

The Ultimate 8502 is ready for action with a 2.6-inch touch screen, QWERTY keyboard; integrated GPS; Windows Mobile 6 Professional software; an XGA video out capability; and i-Q services for remote device management.

i-mate Ultimate 8150

Designed for busy professionals on the go, the Ultimate 8150 includes a touch screen, a keypad, Windows Mobile 6 Professional, XGA video out capability, and i-Q services for remote device management.

i-mate Ultimate 6150

Designed for busy professionals on the go, the Ultimate 6150 runs Windows Mobile 6 Professional and includes a 2.8-inch VGA touch screen; XGA video out capability; and i-Q services for remote device management.

i-mate JAMA 201

Running Windows Mobile software and featuring a 2.5-inch, full-color screen, the JAMA 201 is ready for business.

i-mate JAMA 101

The JAMA 101 provides powerful Windows Mobile 6.0 Professional functionality in a compact, light, and easy-to-use phone.

In addition to the above products i-mate™ offers:

1. Big business benefits

2. Phone customization

3. Security solutions using the PC

4. Online help and service centers at various regions

5. Enterprise solutions which include CRM and account management

6. Touch screen technology

7. Chinese and Japanese language assistance

6.0.2 Price

Product

Ultimate 9502	$974.00
Ultimate 8502	$599.00
Ultimate 8150	$624.00
Ultimate 6150	$624.00
JAMA 201	$393.19
JAMA 101	$349.00

Comparatively, the Palm® Treo™ Pro has a QWERTY keyboard and is on sale for $AU599.00. The Ultimate 9502, 6150 and Jama 201 also have QWERTY keyboards. i-mate™ is not under-cutting competition on prices.

6.0.3 Promotion

Sales promotion and purchasing online is done direct through the i-mate™ website and also indirectly through distributors in the allotted geographical market segments. Promotion is also done through the Microsoft website showing smartphone options, alongside other suppliers, although online, purchasing is done directly through i-mate™. As new products enter the market the promotion of these will be tailored to the region.

6.0.4 Place

The following geographical locations have target market access to i-mate™:

- Middle East
- Australasia
- Africa
- Italy
- UK
- Rest of Europe
- North America
- Asia

Service Centers are available throughout these locations. In addition to the above, i-mate™ intends to pursue emerging markets in India and Russia. A direct online channel is also widely used and available.

7.0 Summary

In summary, this report has provided i-mate™ with an analysis of the market and critiques its international marketing strategy. i-mate™ short and long term branding strategies have been recommended, as well as public relations steps to improve brand equity. Finally, an overview of the marketing mix has been provided.

Health Care Product

Highlights of this Marketing Plan:
1. NPV and IRR are used in Financial Analysis
2. Financial Sensitivity Analysis is included
3. Detailed IMC discussion

1.0 Executive Summary

HairRepair is a hair restoration and therapeutic follicle regeneration system corporately headquartered in New York, NY. HairRepair brings a unique and transformational product for businesses and consumers in the marketplace. The company offers emerging technologically advanced LED light energy therapy for men and women that are experiencing hair loss. The product can be used by customers inconspicuously and without the rigorous application of topically invasive products and/or oral prescriptions. HairRepair is the designer and manufacturer of our products and perform all product design and manufacturing within the US.

Mission Statement:

To strive to develop a superior Hair Replacement Product for our customers through state-of-the-art technology, innovation, leadership and integrity. Trust and believe in the magic of the marketplace; and maintain an open line of communication that listens to new ideas and offers support to both consumers and employees alike.

2.0 Product Description:

HairRepair works as a consumer hair restoring mechanism that uses LED light therapy to rejuvenate hair follicles at the cellular level within the comfort of their own home. It is designed to increase circulation to the scalp area rejuvenating follicles through photo-therapy with minimal side effects. The product is a minimally invasive, head worn skull cap that is outfitted with 400 LED lights and customers that follow the daily program guidelines, including shampoo and lotion, can see an increased growth of hair. LED therapy has been proven to rejuvenate skins cells but has never before been used to grow hair although FDA has approved LED therapy for hair.

LED is Light-Emitting Diode which is a semi-conductor infrared light source. When a diode is forward biased (switched on), electrons are able to recombine with holes within the device, releasing energy in the form of photons. This photon light therapy is the scientific application of light to specific points to activate or produce particular physiological results. In this case, it stimulates the follicles to produce hair growth in otherwise dormant hair roots.

The prototype unit is 7.25 in diameter in the form of a skull cap or baseball hat, but the unit is a custom fit product based on the needs of the consumer. Battery powered with 3 AAA batteries energize the 400 strategically placed infrared lights (lights are 1cm diameter each) but can be sourced through alternative A/V cable.

3.0 Target Demographic:

HairRepair is a specialized product. Healthy male or female private sector consumers, between the ages of 16-70, that have experienced hair loss or reduction in the amount of hair over time (receding hairline or through genetic pattern). Target customer is specialized, urban, intellectual and educated. Ideal customer should be in the middle income demographic ($40,000/yr + annually) with robust disposable and discretionary income

4.0 SWOT Analysis:

4.1 Strengths

- Direct Sales to customers and on-site customer service
- First of a kind, creating the ability open as the market leader.
- Technologically advanced

4.2 Weaknesses

- Little or no market presence, consumer response unknown
- Lack solid dealer or distributor relationship

4.3 Opportunities

- No clear market leader, strong brand names, or reputations

4.4 Threats

- Taxes
- Lack of high capital reserves

5.0 Competitive Analysis

5.1 **ABC Laser Hair Comb** is a Japanese hair comb manufactured to use for hair loss that uses LED therapy. The ABC Laser Comb is a joint development with the Medical Laser Research Center, University of Tokyo, Japan.

ABC is a subsidiary of **DFE Medical Inc.,** a Singapore based company. **DFE Medical** develops manufacturers and also distributes a range of Low Power Laser (LLLT) and Light Emitting Diode (LED) therapy devices in both consumer and medical market. Lasers and LED technology is currently being researched in a broad spectrum of cosmetics applications including, but not limited to hair and scalp restoration, permanent hair removal, treatment of acne and anti-aging procedures.. DFE claims they were founded to increase public awareness of the benefits of Lasers and LED technology and to provide devices that are safe, effective and affordable.

5.2 **Rogaine** (Minoxidil) **and Propecia** (Finasteride) are two drugs are available for the treatment of balding in men. Rogaine (Minoxidil), a topical product, is available without a prescription in two strengths. Propecia (Finasteride) is a prescription drug taken orally once daily to treat male pattern baldess. Rogaine is manufactured and distributed by McNeil-PPC a subsidiary of Johnson & Johnson. Propecia is manufactured and distributed by Merck & Co. Inc Pharmaceuticals. Propecia has also been cleared by the FDA to treat prostate cancer and enlarged prostate(BPH) in males. Rogaine can also double as a vasodialator in treatment for high blood pressure. For this analysis, these products are typically used for regrowing hair in customers who have gradually thinning hair or gradual hair loss on the top of the head.

5.3 Disadvantages to using Competitor's product

- Results vary and are no longer visible when product discontinued
- Dangerous to small animals and children
- Not recommend for use with women.
- Minoxidil may cause increased growth or darkening of fine body hairs
- Hair loss instead of hair growth
- Dry, itchy and irritated skin
- Inconvenience of daily routine
- Fast Moving Consumer Goods(FMCG)

5.4 Disadvantages in using *HairRepair* vs Competitor

- Lack of financial strength of a parent company.
- No brand identity.
- Larger perceived upfront investment for customer
- Initial marketing expense to ensure market penetration

6.0 Financial Analysis

6.1 Break Even Analysis

Fixed Costs

- Office Space - $1200/mo
- Salaries - $1000/mo
- Phones - - $125/mo
- Insurance - $425/mo
- Marketing/Adv - $1000/mo

Variable Costs

- Direct Materials - $12.75/per unit
- Materials - $29.50/per unit
- Utilities - $15.00/per unit

  ** Unit priced at $199.99

  BE = Fixed Cost / Contribution Margin
  = $3750 / ($199.99- $57.25)
  = $3750 / $142.74
  = 26.27 units

6.2. Net Present Value Analysis

The current Discount Rate as determined by the Federal Reserve is 5.25%. Prime interest rate is 5.625% .The initial investment out of pocket to capitalize HairRepair is estimated at $120,000. The capital expenditure is taking into consideration initial product costs, leases, down payments, and payroll costs incurred before sales begin. Using a safe hypothesis based on current market conditions, it must be conservatively assumed that between year 1 and 2 will have 0% revenue growth from the beginning FY. This is based on the lump sum outgo of the initial investment and startup costs associated with a new business the first year. Startup cost that will not be present the following years as business revenues grow.

Discount Rate................ 5.25%
Est. Project Life..............10 years
Investment................... $120,000

Year	No of Units	Sold Revenue
1	360	71996.00
2	360	71996.00
3	368	73596.00
4	379	75796.00
5	379	75796.00
6	398	79596.00
7	426	85195.00
8	460	91995.00
9	496	99195.00
10	535	106994.00

Net Present Value: $502,896.78

PV of Expected Cash Flows: $622,896.78

> IRR= 57.992%
>
> With a discount rate of 5.25% and a span of 10 years, projected cash flows are worth $622,896.78 today, which is greater than the initial $120,000.00 paid. The resulting positive NPV of the project is $502,896.78, which indicates that pursuing the business venture is optimal from an investment standpoint.

6.3 Financial Sensitivity Analysis

HairRepair is a product that is subject to the ebbs and flows of market conditions. Sensitivity analysis allows for the opportunity to quantify uncertainty in best and worst case value. Several variables should be considered as having the potential to affect NPV.

- Change in Discount Rate
- Improvements in Technology
- Taxation
- Unforeseen expenses

	Expected	Pessimistic	Optimistic
Beginning Cash Balance	$120,000	$120,000	$120,000
Cash Inflows (Income):			
Accounts Receivables	65,996	59,396	72,596
Sales & Receipts	5,999	5,399	6,599
S&H Charges	3,600	3,240	3,960
Sales Tax 8.1%	5,345	4,811	5,880
Total Cash Inflows	$80,940	$72,846	$89,035
	$200,940	$192,846	$209,035
Cash Outflows (Expenses):			
Advertising	$12,000	$12,000	$12,000
Bank Service Charges	200	220	180
Insurance	5,100	5,100	5,100
Inventory Purchases	20,000	20,000	20,000
Licenses & Permits	175	175	175
Office	0	0	0
Payroll	10,800	11,880	9,720
Payroll Taxes	1,080	1,180	972
Rent or Lease	12,000	12,000	12,000
Repairs & Maintenance	1,000	1,100	900
Supplies	400	440	360
Sales Tax	5,345	4,811	5,880
Utilities & Telephone	1,000	1,000	1,000
Subtotal	$69,100	$69,906	$68,287
Other Cash Out Flows:			
Capital Purchases	$3,000	$3,000	$3,000
Decorating	$300	$330	$270
Fixtures & Equipment	$2,000	$2,200	$1,800
Owner's Draw	$12,000	$12,000	$12,000
Other:			
Subtotal	$17,300	$17,530	$17,070
Total Cash Outflows	$86,410	$87,436	$85,357
Ending Cash Balance	$114,530	$105,410	$123,678

1st Year Sensitivity Analysis (+/- 10%)

7.0 Product Pricing Structure
$199.99 unit price
P(199.99) – VC(57.25) = **$142.74 Unit Contribution Margin**

7.1 Pricing and Marketing Mix

Pricing: HairRepair is priced using *Perceived-Value Pricing Method*. Over time, customers that have experienced hair loss go through many of the same frustrations as customers in the weight loss industry. It is not uncommon for a consumer to try 8-10 products with little success, looking for a solution to the problem of pattern hair loss. The lack of a "bona-fide" successful product in the market coupled with the growing number of citizens more concerned with appearance, adds to a high perceived value in a product that is new, has FDA clearance, and will work. Moreover, strengths of the operation lie in the delivery of customer service, support, warranties, product performance and the overall trust relationship.

- Customer Service price premium - $60
- Warranty price premium - $60
- Product price premium - $20
- Support price premium - $50
- New product image premium - $10

     TOTAL $200

Distribution:
HairRepair plans to employ a Direct-to-Consumer distribution sales channel. The product will be available through the website and through various e-commerce outlets. As business levels dictate, the future plan is to add various strategic retailers as well. HairRepair realizes the initial disadvantage to limited distribution channels. There will be a strong emphasis on customer satisfaction, value-added services, order accuracy, on-time shipments and corresponding operating expenses to offset initial market competitive disadvantage.

Advertising/Promotion:
Several different advertising efforts will be employed including internet ads, radio spots, and direct mail to target market.

Customer Service:
HairRepair will work to achieve an optimal level of customer care and support. The company will engage in a management philosophy that closes the gap between customer expectations and ultimate satisfaction with the end result. The goal is to keep customer service issues to a minimum that are the result unrealized customer perceptions of the end results provided by the product. The delivery of this information is rooted in communication and information. Also, maintaining a philosophy of customer recovery when complaints arise by empowering employees to take the steps necessary to "make it right".

Year	Unit Sales	Revenue	FC/VC	Gross Profit
1	360	71996.00	63810.00	E*
2	360	71996.00	63810.00	8186.00
3	368	73596.00	64228.00	9368.00

3yr Estimate
E*($8186.00) Denotes reinvestment back in to Cash on Hand

8.0 Channels of Distribution
At the present time, HairRepair will not use Distribution Channels but rather a direct-to-

customer approach. This will allow for costs to remain low as market penetration takes place and Brand Identity is raised. As business levels grow, room would be made to expand and partner with channels to obtain a larger reach. It would then make better financial sense to employ a department that is geared toward sales, training and equipping intermediaries. Direct marketing also allows monitoring and gauging marketing efforts because the relationship between a campaign and the sales that result from it can be evaluated. Moreover, the benefits of direct communication with end-users is vital to obtain organizational and product feedback.

The sales, support, inventory and manufacturing components(50% wool/50% cotton cap, 400 LED red lights, adjustable notch, shampoo, A/C adapter, battery pack) of the delivery process will all be completed within the same office facility. A customer can order a product two ways: (1) Online through the webpage and (2) through the toll free phone number. The sales-to-consumer flow is as follows:

1. Contact is made with HairRepair Sales in response to Ad

2. Sales is made and size and customer information is obtained

3. Payment (incl $10 shipping and handling)

4. HairRepair Cap is custom manufactured using existing inventory

5. Product shipped to customer (5-7days)

6. Follow up with customer to obtain feedback.

9.0 Integrated Marketing Communication

HairRepair's goal to create an IMC is to develop a network of marketing channels with an emphasis in e-commerce, Press releases, social media, and promotions. The 2 major components of the system are Internet marketing, and direct marketing interfaces. The goal of HairRepair in using IMC in its marketing efforts is to create a harmonious message to consumers through all channels. That message is: *HairRepair is focused on developing a growing network of consumers and business relationships that creates loyalty and offers a value based product.* There is a long-term goal to add other channels such as TV, Radio and Billboards as business levels necessitate

9.1 Internet
- **Website Design**

   HairRepair will create and maintain an interactive webpage complete with Company information, Product information and History, Online Transaction Processing, Feedback Forums and Contact information - **$500 set up design/ $45 mo.**

- **Email Blasts**

  Comprehensive email blasts are imperative to creating an initial "buzz" of awareness within local circles, friends and family. Accompanying word of mouth information between friends and colleagues is helpful as well. Coupons and promotions can be sent this way to help persuade potential customers with mass emailed ads 2x a month - **$400 CAD design of ad.**

- **Social Media**

  The use of Facebook and Twitter accounts have become effective social mediums to network with a broad range of consumers at very little cost. The use of this channel allows for HairRepair to reach consumers via personal profiles, groups, fan pages and events.

- **Banner Ads on Specific Websites**

  The most common banner size used to be 468 x 60 pixels (Full Banner. The ads are also helpful in the tracking of consumer behavior through the use of "Cookies". Cookies also allow an advertiser to catalog which banner ad a visitor saw that brought him to the advertiser's site, and which banner ads resulted in actual sales. The typical website HairRepair would target would be News and sports based webpages and internet search engines to reach to maximum amount of the target market. Pricing is based on "views" and "click-thru". **$350 ad design/ $200 for 10,000 views/ 10 sales(based on 1% ROR) at $50 per sale $500= $1050 first month/ $700 ea additional month.**

9.2 Direct Marketing

- **Direct mail**

  A direct mail campaign can accomplish 2 objectives for HairRepair. (1) Create an awareness in the community and (2) Offer consumer discounts on products. Direct mailing a coupon allow the company to accurately target the appropriate consumers that would benefit from the product. The ad coupon would consist of a 5x8 cardstock offering a 15% discount and a FREE consultation at no obligation. It would also ad a caveat that the first 10 customers that resond would get a unit FREE to try and wirte an evaluation. The ad would be **$750 per 1000 pc mailer done ever other month.**

- **Local Newspapers and Publications**

  A 1/8 page ad in the Sports section of the local paper in New York is **$380** 1x per week Black and White incl design. Budgeting allows HairRepair to run an ad 2x per month on Sundays. Total Cost at **$760/mo. Every other month**

10.0 Summary of IMC Budget

FY (1) IMC Budget:	$12,000.00
Website Design/Updates:	$995.00
PR Press Release:	$50.00
Email blast CAD design:	$400.00
Banner Ad (est.):	$1050.00
Direct Mail pc.:	$4500.00
Newspaper Ad:	$4560.00
TOTAL:	$11,555.00
Budget Surplus:	$445.00

11.0 Conclusion

The proposed medical product, HairRepair, is going to bring in a 10-year NPV of $503K using a discount rate of 5.25%, indicating an optimal business venture as compared to similar business projects in the same sector. The sales and marketing expenses are expected to total $11.5K in the first year of launch, with the majority of spending on direct mail and print advertising in newspapers.

Outdoor Lighting

Highlights of this Marketing Plan:
1. Executive Summary is well drafted
2. Good SWOT analysis
3. A balanced discussion on Marketing Mix

Executive Summary

The mission of GardenBright is to create safe, environmentally friendly products that are economical for consumers. GardenBright does not want to break the bank for consumers, so the product is well priced slightly above electrical competition. The product has a positive impact on the environment, as it requires just the UV rays from the sun to function, and is made and packaged in completely recycled materials.

One main goal for the GardenBright is to be the name consumers ask for when they go to purchase their outdoor lighting in retail locations. Another goal for the company is to expand past the consumer market into the commercial market, specifically in restaurants with outdoor seating.

GardenBright is a company that produces outdoor rail lighting to the consumer market that requires the use of solar energy with the target market being residential homeowners with an outdoor living space. GardenBright has found that there is a lot of consumer demand for the lighting product, but on the other hand there are already plenty of existing outdoor lighting brands in the marketplace, tough for brand awareness. One of the main competitors of GardenBright is NightBulb LED lighting among various solar post cap companies. GardenBright is expected to have first year sales of $1,350,000 in 2011 and increase by over 50% in sales over the next three years. GardenBright will be distributed via two-step distribution channel at a price to wholesaler of $45 per unit (set of four lights per one unit) with a suggested retail price to the consumer of $95. The promotional budget for 2011 is $258,273 and includes a mix of print and online media directly from the company and an allotment for retailers for local advertising. GardenBright has found that there is a lot of consumer demand for the lighting product, but on the other hand there are already plenty of existing outdoor lighting brands in the marketplace, tough for brand awareness.

The recent recession in the market over the past few years has created consumers to look for ways to save the money that they have and change the ways they were spending. This has caused consumers to travel less and use their own backyards as a staycation. Whatever their outdoor space is, consumers are looking for ways to create their own personalized outdoor living space from different decking material, to patio décor, and outdoor lighting.

Over the next three years GardenBright anticipates sales to more than double with market awareness brought down through distribution channels and by advertising directly to contractors and consumers.

Product Description

GardenBright lighting, located in New York, NY is a lighting system designed for outdoor railings that is powered through sunlight. The material and packaging used for the GardenBright product is 90% recycled content. The system may be installed within the rails, rail posts, or stair risers of a deck to offer additional outside lighting, as well as a unique look and feel to any outdoor living space. GardenBright solves two of the main problems for consumers who want to add lighting to their outdoor living space.

Consumers want to have outdoor lighting but do not want to increase their electricity bill with the cost of running current LED rail lighting systems that require transformers. GardenBright gives consumers the opportunity to add outdoor lighting without breaking the bank every month because there is no electricity required to run the lighting system. The LED electrical rail lighting systems that are available in the market currently are required to be installed when the railing unit is installed, which limits the consumer to add a lighting system to an existing railing unit without taking the entire railing apart. The solar lighting system can be installed with a new railing unit or to a pre-existing railing unit while leaving the railing intact.

Secondly, the only solar lighting system for railings is solar post caps which limits the amount of light available and customization. The GardenBright system allows consumers to customize entire rail sections to offer a unique look compared to neighbors, and more locations to have solar lighting instead of just on top of posts.

Some of the challenges that GardenBright faces include increasing competition, budgeting, and distribution channels. Outdoor lighting has become an increasingly popular trend over the past couple of years and with that comes an increase in competition that want a piece of the market share. GardenBright is a new startup company and being privately held needs investors to support the company and budget to successfully launch the product and to get consumers aware of the brand. The company is in a mixed mindset as to which way would be the most successful way to distribute the product; selling GardenBright online exclusively or through a two-step distribution channel. GardenBright is fearful it will lose its two-step partners who have exclusivity in their respective territories if the product is available online to anyone.

Strengths

- Innovative product
- There are other solar lighting products, but not that can be built into the rail.
- Consumer Demand
- Outdoor lighting is increasing in popularity.
- Location
- Company is located in the heard of target market.
- Environmentally conscious
- Green products and energy saving products are gaining favorability among consumers.

Weaknesses
- Price
- Price point is high due to new product to market.
- Brand Loyalty
- As a startup company, consumers are unaware of the brand.
- Budget
- Product launch requires a lot of capital to successfully market.
- Distribution Channels
- Conflicting between strictly sales online or a two-step channel.

Opportunities
- Merger
- Company could merge with a larger railing manufacturer
- Commercial market
- Condominium associations, outdoor restaurants, and marinas.
- Huge market for outdoor living
- With the current economy, people are vacationing less and creating a 'staycation' in their back yard.
- International
- Possible to expand in other countries.

Threats
- Existing competition
- They have advantage with distribution channels and brand awareness.
- New Competition
- Increase in outdoor lighting competition due to popularity.
- Seasonal business
- Deck building is done in Spring and Summer months due to Winter climate in half of US.
- Weather
- Product function ability with lack of sunlight.

Target Market
The target market for the solar lighting system is residential homeowners who have their

outdoor living space; specifically families with multiple children and retirees. Families with children at home may not have the extra money to go on vacations, so they will improve their outdoor living space to create a customized home oasis. GardenBright gives these families, working adults in their 30's and 40's, the ability to add lighting to customize their deck without increasing their electrical bill every month. Also, retirees, consumers in the "65+ age group" who are no longer working and have grown children that still own houses and are still active and entertaining family and guests at their home. Homeowners can include townhouse or condominium owners that typically cannot change the outdoor features of their home due to being a part of an association.

Geographically, GardenBright is primary targeting the Mid and South Atlantic states (New Jersey through Florida) and with the location of the company in New York, NY they are close to the market. This geographic market was chosen based upon weather and where the majority of decks are being built year round. In New England and the Midwestern states, the cold wind and snow prevents deck and rail use and installation during the Fall and Winter months. The deck building and usage season is typically in the late Spring and Summer months for those states. Eventually GardenBright would like to move into those markets as well, but as a new product would like to specifically focus on warmer climate states where deck installation and enjoyment is year round. As distribution for GardenBright increases, the company would also like to target the Southwestern states and Southern California because of year round warm climates as well, but since the company is currently located on the East Coast they would like to focus on that region.

As GardenBright achieves brand recognition in its target market, the company would like to explore other avenues in commercial applications and international distribution. Management feels that the product would do well marketing as a safety feature for restaurants and ski lodges with outdoor patio seating as well as provide a certain ambiance to set the mood for clientele. They are currently researching for a test site for feedback from the restaurant employees and customers. GardenBright would like to market the safety feature for condominiums, but needs to explore if there is a real need for that type of application, and if the price would fit into an association budget. Internationally, management believes the product would do well in commercial applications, but needs to investigate effective distribution as shipping products overseas increases the price drastically.

Competitive Analysis

Two main competitors for GardenBright include NightBulb LED Lighting and DEF Solar Caps.

NightBulb is an LED under rail lighting system that is powered by a transformer. The transformer can hold up to 80 lights and requires to be plugged into an electrical outlet. The lights are sold in packs of four retailing at $70 per pack and the transformers sold separately at $128 each. NightBulb is a product of ABC Enterprise and is only meant to be installed with ABC's railing system, RailWays. This product is sold through lumberyards across the country that carries ABC decking products as well as online at HomeDepot.com. So, the product is well distributed in the US. A three-year warranty is offered for the LED lights and a one-year warranty for the transformer from the date of installation offered by the manufacturer. This product is the only product currently on the market that offers customization with the amount of lights that are underneath the rail, but requires the use of electrical transformers, which can increase monthly electrical bill. This product is well distributed, but a huge disadvantage is that it is only meant to be installed with RailWays Railing at the time of installation, so consumers are limited to using that type of railing. NightBulb is available online at homedepot.com whereas RailWays Railing is not, so the consumer can order the lighting but the railing may not be available to them. GardenBright can be installed with any type of railing system and can be installed after the rail was originally installed, so this is a great advantage to NightBulb limited to being installed with one railing product. GardenBright lighting will also cut back on the consumer's electrical bill while providing the same customization and clean look that NightBulb offers.

Once GardenBright is available, ABC Enterprise may want to look at redesigning the installation of NightBulb because it is most likely that NightBulb is a bonus selling feature for their RailWays railing product; consumers purchase RailWays because it's their only option of have LED lighting on their rails. Since GardenBright can be installed with any decking product; ABC Enterprise may not only lose NightBulb sales but RailWays sales as well. Since NightBulb is the only product of its kind currently available, it will feel the effect of a new competitor with attractive advantages.

There are many different companies that offer a mix of decorative and solar post caps, but DEF Solar Caps strictly sells solar post caps online. Currently, solar post caps are the only solar offering for railing that is a part of the rail system. DEF Solar Caps offers their solar post caps exclusively online for customer order through their website. These caps can be used with any type of railing such as wood or vinyl and can be used with any brand so the customer is not limited in which type of railing they have for this product. The caps range in price from $28 to $33 each which the price point is set directly in the middle of the $19 to $63 price range for solar post caps available at homedepot.com. The advantage that GardenBright has over DEF Solar Caps along with the other solar post cap companies currently in the market is that customers are allowed to customize their rails with more than just solar lighting on their post caps but also underneath their rails and on stair risers. GardenBright offers more of a lighting solution and customization for the backyard without the use of electricity. Another advantage to GardenBright is if it is sold through a two-step distribution channel the product will be available in retail locations and in front of the consumer to see and touch in person instead of just online.

Since there are already so many solar post cap products available in the market; the introduction of GardenBright will not have a direct effect on DEF Solar Caps. It may introduce a similar product to compete with GardenBright since they have had presence in the market for about 10 years and hold a position with market share.

GardenBright will be distributed through a two-step distribution system through wholesalers and dealers. As a new product on the market this will be the best way to get GardenBright in the faces of the consumer. After looking at the benefits of selling directly through an online store, it's a gamble because there is no way for the consumer to see the product in person and how it actually works before purchasing.

Financial Analysis

The following is a three year sales forecast for GardenBright; the company is predicting a 30% increase in sales from 2011 to 2012 and a 50% increase in sales from 2012 to 2013 as the product becomes more available in the market and demand increases.

Three Year Sales Forecast			
	2011	2012	2013
Sales $	$1,350,000	$1,755,000	$2,632,500
Units Sold	30,000	39,000	58,500

Sales Price to Wholesaler	$45
Direct Material + Marketing	$20.00
Direct Labor	$5.00
Contribution Margin	$20.00
Yearly fixed costs	$500,000
Break Even Sales Volume	25,000

3-Year Sales Forecast and Break Even Analysis

For GardenBright to cover costs in year one the company needs to sell 25,000 GardenBright kits before it will begin to make a profit. GardenBright is forecasted to sell 30,000 units in year one to wholesalers, so it is anticipated to sell 5,000 more units than the break-even amount.

Sales Price to wholesaler	$45	30,000	$1,350,000
Direct Material + Marketing	$20.00	30,000	$600,000
Direct Labor	$5.00	30,000	$150,000
Total Variable Costs			$750,000
Contribution Margin			$600,000
Fixed Cost	$500,000		$500,000
Net Income			$100,000

Income Statement 2011

$$NVP = \$100,000 + \$500,000/\$20.00 = 30,000 \text{ units need to be sold to make a } \$100,000$$
$$\text{profit in 2011.}$$

Since GardenBright is bringing a product to market that is unique and in demand, the company is predicting three good initial years since the company is forecasted to produce a profit and increase in profit over the three years. Normally, the first few years of business, companies tend to take a loss or barely breakeven because their costs outweigh debt to initial lack of sales. A bad scenario would be GardenBright continually taking a loss over the first few years and running the risk of filing bankruptcy or closing its doors because it spent too much money before starting to make money.

Product Pricing Structure

GardenBright will be sold in a pack of four solar lights and sold to wholesalers at $45 per unit. The $45 allows room for the wholesaler to mark up and make a profit to the retailer and the retailer to the homeowner at a suggested retail price of $95 per unit. The $95 per unit to the consumer gives leeway for the wholesaler and retailer to charge a 25-30% markup and cover any shipping or inventory charges.

The pricing strategy used to develop the price for GardenBright was Skimming Pricing. GardenBright is a unique product on the market and the company feels it is able to initially charge a premium price because of the benefits it offers in comparison to completive products available in the market. NightBulb is sold for $70, but then the consumer must pay additionally in their electricity bill over time and replacement of LED bulbs. GardenBright is a high price to consumers, but it is a onetime feel since the system is powered by the sun. One unit of GardenBright at $95 will cover 4-8 feet of rail depending on how far the lights are spaced apart, but depending on how large the patio is and if lights are installed elsewhere, the cost per unit can add up.

Based upon the financial analysis, projected revenues for the first year for GardenBright is $1,350,000 with a net profitability of $100,000. With this pricing structure GardenBright will see an increase in sales in year two by 30% and in year three by 50%.

Channels of Distribution

GardenBright believes more initial sales will result from a two-step distribution system, and will evaluate direct online selling again after the first year. The promotional focus will be a mix between directly to consumers as well as to wholesalers, retailers, and contractors to generate market awareness. The focus will mainly be directed the consumer via PULL System up the distribution channel. Consumers will inquire about GardenBright at their local lumberyard, which will in turn create demand for the product. Local lumberyards will then contact their distributors in the area that will in turn cause the distributors to contact GardenBright directly.

GardenBright will be manufactured in New York, NY, and as a small package inventory can easily be stored right at the manufacturing facility. Wholesalers' who distribute GardenBright can easily store inventory in their warehouses due to the small package size and shipping costs are very inexpensive. GardenBright will provide its channel members with the tools that will allow them to successfully carry the product. All displays and literature will be at no cost to the lumberyards that carry GardenBright; they will just have to pay for the shipping of the marketing pieces. By having the lumberyards pay for shipping on marketing materials will enable them to only order what they need and keep costs down.

GardenBright will begin with one independent manufacturer's representative for the first year. This person will be responsible for outside customer relations and will receive a monthly salary plus a commission based upon sales. Due to the fact that he/she will be an independent representative of the company, GardenBright will save on expense costs for the representative. The sales rep will be a direct contact for all wholesaler and dealer relations with the support of the inside sales team. He/she is responsible for product knowledge and training, as well as making sure retail locations are stocked with the necessary displays and literature.

Integrated Marketing Communication

The primary objective for GardenBright promotional efforts is to get greaten consumer awareness of the product and to create consumer demand at the retail level. The consistent message that will be portrayed to the consumer is that there are other alternatives to outdoor lighting that can save money and are better for the environment.

The advertising mix for GardenBright will include the following:

Print media:

GardenBright will advertise in a mix of publications to pull the consumer and contractor to the retailer and to push the product down the chain by advertising to the wholesale and retail level. Consumer publications are the most expensive to place ads in, but GardenBright feels that this is an important cost to generate consumer product awareness.

> *Regional* – GardenBright will allocate a certain percentage of sales to help out retail locations with the cost of advertising GardenBright in local newspapers and publications
>
> *National* – Full page ads 3x a year will run in national deck and patio publications geared toward consumers such as Better Homes and Gardens Special Interest Publications.

Radio/TV:

GardenBright will allocate a certain percentage of sales to contribute to local advertisements that retailers run with GardenBright, but will not promote the product directly through those media.

Social Media:
GardenBright will have links from its website to Facebook and Twitter pages where fans can post pictures of GardenBright in use and stay up to date with company information. You Tube videos will be provided on the website with installation information.

Other Internet:
GardenBright will be included in online e –newsletters for contractor and wholesale/retail websites, and will be listed on architectural websites such as 4specs.com. 4specs.com is a great website that is basically one stop shopping for architects when they are looking for products to spec for any upcoming building projects

Direct Marketing:
GardenBright has done some online research of decking and railing manufacturers and has acquired dealer and contractor customer contact information directly from their websites. With the email addresses that have been acquired, GardenBright will send out product email blasts to these potential customers.

Personal Selling:
GardenBright will initially have one independent manufacturer sales rep for the initial geographic target. Hiring an independent rep will save the company money initially for benefits and salary because the rep will incur all expenses such as vehicle and meals. This will help open more doors at the retail and wholesale level because of the other product lines he/she represents.

Public Relations:
Public Relations will be handled in house for the first year to save the cost of monthly agency fees Initial releases include a general company and product introduction including all the benefits. GardenBright is a green product since it does not require the use of electricity, so using the product qualifies for LEED points in residential building applications.

Overview of IMC Budget
Print media: $2,000
Radio/TV: $5,000
Social Media: $500
Online Advertisements: $1,000
Direct Marketing: $2,000
Personal Selling: $2,500
Public Relations: $500

Total (year 1): $13,500

Conclusion

GardenBright is an environmentally friendly outdoor lighting product that is economical for consumers. This product is going to bring in $100K net income in the first year of operation, with 30,000 units sold to wholesalers, which is 5K units over the break-even requirement. The sales and marketing expenses are expected to total $13.5K in the first year of launch, with the majority of spending on Radio/TV ads and Personal Selling activities.

Chapter 6 –
Marketing Plan Example –
Business Services

Financial Consulting Service

Highlights of this Marketing Plan:
1. Service Description is well drafted
2. Good target market discussion
3. Detailed financials

Executive Summary

ASFCN Consultants is every small business owner's one stop to a complete business analysis including an in depth look at the company's financial processes, accounting processes, marketing techniques, and human resources. ASFCN Consultants also provides both business and individual tax preparation services. Each business that we consult will receive a detailed business plan that will help each business owner operates their company more efficiently and more profitably. ASFCN Consultants prides ourselves on the ability to provide our customers with all the support services necessary to improve.

In an area where there are thousands of small businesses, we plan on reaching out to these companies to assist them in their day-to-day functioning. We are the only company that provides our customers with multiple services, and we plan to reach out to struggling companies. We provide our customers with competitive pricing, and provide each customer with the luxury of us traveling to their location for an analysis. This will prevent the business from further disruption.

We at ASFCN, associates will work to meet or exceed the expectations from our customers, and provide them with premium quality service, tailored specifically for their individual needs

ASFCN Consultants Product Plan

ASFCN Consultants is a company that places our customers at the forefront of our operation. Our mission is to assist other small business owners in reaching the level of success they strive to achieve. Since each small business is unique, we will examine all aspects of the organization and develop a comprehensive plan to ensure their accounting, marketing, financial, and human resource obligations are up to date and efficient. ASFCN Consultants' primary focus will be helping small business owners to prioritize the various aspects of their business and help build a solid foundation for them to operate.

Many small business owners struggle to manage a newly formed business while juggling employees and a growing client base. With ever-changing local, state, and federal regulations, it is invaluable to have a competent ally on their team. This is where ASFCN Consultants separates our customers from their competition. There are many consultants available to business owners that provide them feedback on a specific aspect of their business. There are tax consultants that provide business owners with assistance in filing the proper paper work for both their business and their employees at the end of the year. There are financial consultants that look at the way the business allocates their resources. They help to determine where more funds need to be allocated, and where they are spending too much money. Marketing consultants are available to help businesses get their name out and help to expand their clientele. All of these options are available for business owners, but it is not only time consuming but costly for them to get a complete analysis of their business. This is what sets ASFCN Consultants apart from other businesses. With a single phone call, our experienced staff will come in to a business and address all aspects of operations. We are a one-stop solution to this problem. Our services save businesses owners both time and resources.

Our experienced team provides our clients with a broad range of services, most notably advanced tax specialists and years of personal experience owning and operating successful companies of varying sizes. Our mission is to allocate our time to gain a complete understanding of our customers' businesses. Our team will review everything from hiring, to accounting, marketing, to customer service. We will do an advanced study of time management and form a report as to how efficiently the company is operating day-to-day. With a complete and thorough understanding of the business, we will be able to develop a business plan, which will give business owners guidelines as to how to expand their business as well as operate more efficiently. Rather than seeking out multiple consultants, our company strives to address all of the concerns that small business owners have.

Our staff is highly trained in tax preparation, and because of this, we expect that much of our tax preparation services will be from businesses that we consult. We will also be offering our tax preparation services for individuals and families, as we see this as an opportunity to further our business without compromising our consulting services.

There is no doubt that our company will face challenges along the way. The economy in the United States is struggling, and small businesses are facing high levels of taxation as well as changing regulations. With these challenges working against us, many businesses may not have the resources to seek out our assistance. We will make it our goal to assure our customers that the services we provide are invaluable and will result in higher profitability after upon the completion of our consultation. We also may find that single service consultants in the area may be strong competitors to our business. We recognize that many small business owners only believe that they need assistance in a single aspect of their business, and it may be a challenge to make them recognize the importance of our services. We will market our business to address these challenges and reassure our customers that an in-depth look into the business will result in the most effective business plan to further their successes.

ASFCN Consultants concentrates on marketing to businesses in the New York area. Since the services we provide are on a one-on-one basis, it will be imperative that we be able to meet and interact with the business owner as well as become involved in the day-to-day operations. With our small staff, it will be important for us to operate locally to ensure prompt responses to our customer's requests. Because of the services we provide, we prefer to service business with less than 25 employees. This will help to ensure that we can do a complete and thorough analysis of each business in a timely manner. There are no consulting businesses in our area offering this varying level of service; therefore, ASFCN Consultants has a market niche unlike any other. Our business is located the Central Business Park of New York. We have an office at this location that is available for customers to come in and meet with our support staff. On site, our staff credentials are available as well as any background information that may be requested. Each customer has the option of meeting with our staff members in our office, or our business can conveniently respond to our customer's location. We strive meet all the demands of our customers, and because our business is primarily based on customer service, we always put our customers first.

S.W.O.T Analysis

Strengths:

- ASFCN Consultants provide customers with full-service, one-on-one attention.

- We devote an extended period of time to individual customers to ensure a complete understanding of the business and how they operate.

- Rather than having an expertise in only one or two facets of business operations, we are skilled in all aspects of starting up and operating a small business.

- There is a low overhead cost for our company, so our prices are competitive for our customers.

- ASFCN Consultants have expertise in tax preparation, as this will be a main source of income for the business.

- Customer care is at the forefront of our priorities.

Weaknesses:

- We have to spend extended periods with business owner to have an understanding of their operations, which ultimately could limit our ability to serve a large client base.

- We do not have a large marketing campaign, so we will be relying heavily on customer satisfaction and word of mouth.

- Because of our one-on-one commitment to our customers, we will not be able to expand our business outside our local area.

- There are not any other all-encompassing companies out there, so customers may not know what they will receive from our services.

- Our customer service requires a lot of one-on-one interaction, so for difficult situations in one business' operations may result in delayed responses to other prospective customers.

- We are unfamiliar with the specifics of many small businesses, so it will be time consuming to gain a familiarity with the operations of each business to be effective.

- Our company is also a small business, so we have a small staff, which may limit our ability to serve a large client base.

Opportunities:

- Our services are personalized for each individual customer.

- As our customer base grows, we expect that our referral base will grow as well.

- Because we are unique in offering a variety of services to our customers rather than expertise in just one area, we expect our customers to take advantage of our extended knowledge.

- With a growing number of small businesses in our general area, our company has the opportunity to expand with the growing small business market.

Threats:

- With a struggling domestic economy, small businesses are facing increased taxation as well as possible mandated insurance coverage that may prevent them from seeking our assistance.

- Many businesses are well known and are experts in a specific area of business operation, so small business owners may seek out only the companies they feel necessary to address inefficiency.

Target Market

ASFCN Consultants has a limited market for our product. Since our business is a service that is based on face-to-face interaction with our customers, our first segmentation in marketing is geographic. The region that our business will be serving will be the New York City area. More specifically, we will be basing our company on an approximately thirty-mile radius around our office located in New York. We recognize that we will be traveling to our customer's business, and in doing so have to account for travel time and be sure that the distance we travel will also be profitable for our company. By setting a thirty-mile radius, this ensures our customers that we will be able to assist them in a timely manner. This radius will also ensure that no extended accommodations will be needed to complete the consultation.

We also will be segmenting our marketing techniques based on the demographic of life stages. Our customers are in a stage of their life where they are opening new small businesses or are already running their own businesses. This is a stage of their life where they will have some serious concerns. Many business owners spend a significant amount of money in order to open their business; therefore, they have a lot riding on the success of their company. Because of this, our company will target new business owners as well as established business owners, providing them with an ally for their operations. Opening a company can be overwhelming, especially at the beginning. Having a viable business plan that the owner can stick to will help alleviate some of the concerns of starting up, as well as allowing business owners to remain profitable throughout the years.

Finally, ASFCN Consultants will be focusing our marketing on a psychographic segmentation. More specifically, we will be focusing our marketing on consumers that are defined as thinkers. With a consumer who is motivated by value, our company would be a great solution for them. Our company provides a valuable service by analyzing other businesses and identifying areas in which they could improve their efficiency. We are also a functional service because we provide a business plan for our customers to follow for a period of time that will make them more successful. Our company focuses on thinkers because they are reflective people who are willing to look at their own business critically in order to improve it. This target market is also responsible, and this is understood, but there is a large amount of responsibility on the shoulders of our customers who are owning and operating businesses.

The last segmentation that our company will be using in terms of marketing is based on the size of the customer's business. Our support staff is small, and because it is time consuming to have a complete understanding of the way the various businesses operate, we will be limiting our target market to businesses that have less than 25 employees. As businesses become larger and larger, it becomes more and more difficult for a consultant to have a clear understanding of all the working parts. By limiting the size, we can assure our customers that we will be able to finish a complete analysis of the business in a timely fashion. This will also ensure me that my company remains profitable.

ASFCN Consultants has a very specific target market. We anticipate that there will be many businesses and business owners that match these characteristics and this will allow our business to expand over time. Our main means of marketing will be through word of mouth from our customers, so we have a commitment to providing our customers with the best service available.

Competitive Analysis

In analyzing possible competitors to ASFCN Consultants, small business consulting firms in our general area who offer similar services are considered. Since we are located in New York, it would be appropriate to explore consulting businesses from New Jersey as well.

The following is a SWOT analysis of the strengths and weaknesses of 2 nearby Business Centres.

ABC Business Centre

Strengths

- State and Federally (SBA) funded program
- Large advertising budget for reaching their target audience
- Satellite locations throughout State of New York
- Able to service large client base, with combined resources of employees
- Have direct connection with New York regulators and are able to refer clients directly to them
- Very informative website, which answers many questions or provides direction to find answers to commonly asked questions

Weaknesses

- Provides their clients with limited personal attention, mostly a generic approach
- Clients have to attend meetings at their office locations, they don't conduct site analysis
- All training and seminars are held at different locations, forcing the client to potentially travel
- As a State funded program, they are not going to turn clients away. More likely than not, clients will not be given direct attention, and questions will go unanswered, or not be answered in a timely manner

DEF Business Centre

Strengths
- State and Federally (SBA) funded program
- Large advertising budget for reaching their target audience
- Satellite locations throughout State of New Jersey
- Able to service large client base, with combined resources of employees
- Have direct connection with New Jersey regulators and are able to refer clients directly to them
- Very informative website, which answers many questions or provides direction to find answers to commonly asked questions
- Satellite location in Washington, and Boston

Weaknesses
- Provides their clients with limited personal attention, mostly a generic approach
- Clients have to attend meetings at their office locations, they don't conduct site analysis
- All training and seminars are held at different locations, forcing the client to potentially travel
- As a State funded program, they are not going to turn clients away. More likely than not, clients will not be given direct attention, and questions will go unanswered, or not be answered in a timely manner

Because both the ABC and DEF Business Centres are state run entities, neither have a profitability analysis available. The services these consulting firms provide are supported by taxpayer money as well as funding from the Federal Government through the Small Business Administration. The purpose of these services is to assist small businesses within their respective states. Both market themselves through state run websites, as well as through referrals from financial institutions and other government agencies.

ASFCN Consultants differs from each of these two competitors since we provide one-on-one consultations with business owners in their workplace. We make every effort to provide flexible meeting times, which is more advantageous for our clients. After meeting with the business owner, we develop a personalized plan to address the questions and concerns of our client. We remain in close contact with our business owners to ensure they stay on track with their progression to meeting their desired goals as outlined in our initial meeting. It is our belief that our customers will benefit from a familiar face supporting them every step of the way. Furthermore, no other competitors provide their customers with the option of having tax preparation as part of their business consulting process. Tax preparation for small businesses is one of the most difficult tasks for an owner. Our ability to assist small business owners with this process will help them yield the greatest returns for their organizations.

Since the only real competitors of ASFCN Consultants are state run entities, there will be no anticipated deviation from their current business practices with the introduction of our company. We intend to work directly with the state organizations in our operations, and possibly benefit from referrals they make to clients who are seeking a higher level of service than what they are able to provide.

Financial Analysis

Product Pricing Structure

- <u>ASFCN Consulting Pricing</u>

  Small Business Consultation Fee = $125 per hour. (Initial consultation is free)

- <u>Federal Tax Preparation</u>

  Costs will vary. These are some of the most commonly filed forms for Federal Tax Returns and their associated fees.

Form	Description	Fee
1040	Individual Tax Return	$130.00
1040A	Individual Tax Return	$120.00
1040EZ	Individual Tax Return	$110.00
1040ES	Estimated Tax Payments	$10.00
Schedule A	Itemized Deductions	$30.00
Schedule B	Interest and Dividend Income	$20.00
Schedule C	Profit or Loss from Business	$75.00
Schedule D	Capital Gains or Losses (each)	$5.00
Schedule E	Supplemental Income and Loss	$50.00
Schedule L	Standard Deductions	$20.00
Schedule SE	Self Employment Tax	$20.00
2106	Employee Business Expense	$20.00
2441	Child and Dependent Care Expense	$20.00
3903	Moving Expenses	$50.00
4562	Depreciation and Amortization	$30.00
6251	Alternative Minimum Tax	$50.00
8283	Non-Cash Charitable Contributions	$20.00
8829	Business Use of the Home	$25.00

New York State Tax Preparation

Form	Description	Fee
1040NY	State of New York Individual Return	$30.00
1040S-NY	State of New York Short Form Return	$20.00

Overview of Tax Preparation Fee

In choosing the pricing strategy for ASFCN Consultants, we determined that the most effective means of pricing would be going-rate pricing. After researching some consulting agencies throughout the United States, it is determined that the cost of business consulting ranged from $80 to $250 per hour. The $125 per hour would be a fair price to charge customers. It is in line with the going rate in the market, if not, cheaper than many business consultants. Because our overhead costs are low, we are able to provide our customers with affordable prices. Again, for our tax preparation services, various accountants are being researched to find out what prices they were charging for their services. There was a wide range of fees that accountants charged their customers, and ASFCN tried to base its fees on the going rate in the market. Both consulting and tax preparation fees are based on market pricing, and in some instances may represent market penetration pricing as a mean to attract new customers.

Projected Gross Revenues

Year One Projections
Small Business Consultation: 14 customers per year (Average of 30 hours per consultation)
    30 hours * $125 per hour = $3,750
    $3,750 * 14 businesses = $52,500

Individual Tax Preparation: 25 customers per year (Average price per filing $150)
    $150 per filing [needs 1.2 hours each] * 25 customers = $3,750

Business Tax Preparation: 15 customers per year (Average price per business $250)
    $250 per filing [needs 2 hours each] * 15 customers = $3,750

Year One Gross Revenue Estimate = $60,000
In our first year of business, it is projected that ASFCN would be able to accept eight small businesses that would request our services for small business consultations. With marketing, and a large number of small businesses, ASFCN's marketing technique would be able to attract at least this many customers. In the worst-case scenario, eight businesses in the first year is expected. Furthermore, it is believed that when the tax time comes, more individuals and businesses alike will choose our services. Between close friends and family, 25 customers is a low estimate for the number of individual tax preparations we would be filing. On top of that, it is believed that friends who are small business owners would also seek out our services along with other businesses who are looking for knowledgeable accountants to take care of the their tax needs. These numbers are based on low expectations and worst-case scenarios.

Year Two Projections
Small Business Consultation: 16 customers per year (Average of 30 hours per consultation)
    30 hours * $125 per hour = $3,750
    $3,750 * 16 businesses = $60,000

Individual Tax Preparation: 25 customers per year (Average price per filing $150)
    $150 per filing * 25 customers = $3,750

Business Tax Preparation: 20 customers per year (Average price per business $250)
    $250 per filing * 20 customers = $5,000

Year Two Gross Revenue Estimate = $68,750
In our second year of business, ASFCN expects that through continued advertising as well

as word of mouth from existing customers, customer base should be able to double over the course of the year. In calculating numbers for the second year, the number for individual tax preparations is expected to remain the same. The worst-case scenario for our tax preparation services is that the same customers from the previous year would return again. For business tax preparations, it is believed that the increase in business consultations will also increase the number of businesses requesting tax preparation.

Year Three Projections
Small Business Consultation: 24 customers per year (Average of 30 hours per consultation)
    30 hours * $125 per hour = $3,750
    $3,750 * 24 businesses = $90,000

Individual Tax Preparation: 25 customers per year (Average cost per filing $150)
    $150 per filing * 25 customers = $3,750

Business Tax Preparation: 25 customers per year (Average cost per business $250)
    $250 per filing * 25 customers = $6,250

Year Three Gross Revenue Estimate - $100,000
In our third year of operation, an increase in the number of small business consultations to 24 is expected while the number of individual tax preparation will be at 25 approximately. ASFCN believes that the increase in the business consultations would also increase the number of businesses requiring business returns.

Breakeven Analysis:

Fixed Costs per Month

Rent	$500.00
Phone/Internet	$50.00
Insurance	$10.00
Other fixed costs	$4000.00
Total Fixed Cost	$4560.00

1 Unit = 1 hour consulting
1 Hour Service Fee = $125.00
Variable costs = $15.00 per hour
Contribution Margin = $125.00 - $15.00 = $110.00
Total Monthly Fixed Costs = $4560
Monthly breakeven = $4560 / 110 ≈ 41 hours in small business consulting

Expected # of chargeable hours in Year 1:

Small Business Consultation: 14 customers /12 months = 1.17 customers per month @ 30 hour each = 35.1 hours.

Individual Tax Preparation: 25 customers / 12 months = 2 customers per month @ 1.2hours each = 2.4 hours

Business Tax Preparation: 15 customers / 12 months = 1.25 customers per month @ 2 hours each = 2.5 hours

Hence, in Year 1, the average # of chargeable hours per month will be 40 hours which almost meet the break even requirement of 41 hours per month. This should not be a concern because starting in Year 2, the expected number of customers will increase significantly to start generating profits for the company.

Channels of Distribution

As a service provider, ASFCN Consultants will be acting as a direct channel service provider. Because we are a service company, we deal directly with our customers in every situation. Our company markets our service directly to our customer with no intermediary. Because of this, we rely heavily on the interactions and bonds that we are able to devise with our customers. It is our mission to take each small business that we interact with and make them both more effective and more profitable.

ASFCN Consultants thrive on being flexible for our customers. Our physical location for our business is in the 123 Central Business Part in New York. Our office is set up as a place for us to meet with potential customers for an initial consultation. We can use this space for meetings in which we address the initial concerns of small business owners. Our office is equipped with a computer, providing Internet access, as well as tons of desk space for us to really engage with our customers. We recognize that small business owners will want to be ensured that they are spending money in an effective manner, and we will have our staff's credentials readily available for our customers. The office will provide a space for us to meet with business owners and explain exactly how we operate and what services we provide.

As convenient as the office is, we also recognize the hectic lifestyles that many small business owners have. Because of this, we try to prevent the owners from being away from their businesses for any period of time, and we provide our customers with the option of our company traveling to them for an initial consultation. We will bring with us all the credentials and necessary equipment for a proper consultation. Our initial meeting will give the business owner and our staff time to get to know each other as well as a time to discuss the business owner's initial concerns about their operations. We will also bring with us some sample materials, providing the business owner physical proof of what they will receive at the completion of our consultation. The sample material will include examples of our marketing plans and analyses, advertising plans, before and after examples of website development and improvement. We will also show examples of competitive analyses, budgeting examples, as wee as profitability and breakeven analyses. We will discuss the procedure for setting goals as well as objectives for the business, and provide the business owner with an example of a final business plan. By providing these examples, the business owner will have tangible evidence of what they will receive at the completion of our consultation.

ASFCN Consultants will be sure to take the time during the initial consultation to explain to the business owner how our company operates. We will explain the daily interaction that will be necessary for our company to have with the customer's and their staff. We will observe the company from open to close from the first day until we have a complete understanding of how the company operates. It is only when we have a total understanding of the company that we will be able to begin performing the analyses necessary to make the business more profitable and effective.

We will also take the time to explain to the business owner that they have choices in terms of what services we will provide. Business owners will have the option of having a complete analysis done of their business, or they can opt to have specific aspects of their businesses analyzed and improved upon. Our flexibility and our ability to provide our customers with tangible evidence of our work will help reassure them that their money will be spent in an effective way.

Integrated Marketing Communications

Since ASFCN Consultants is a relatively new company, advertising will be of utmost importance, especially in the first year. Although much of our promotional campaign for the company will be through personal selling, we plan to promote our service through various mediums to try to reach the widest array of customers. The target market for ASFCN Consultants is any business in the NYC area, with less than twenty-five employees. Thousands of businesses in the area that can benefit from our services and it is our job to attract as many new customers as possible.

First, we will be setting up a website for our business. On the website, we will provide our customers with background information on our staff, as well as information about the services we provide and contact information for our consultations. We will have specific tabs set up for each type of service related to business consulting, as well as a tab set up for our tax preparations. There will be a plethora of information on the website so that possible customers are aware of exactly what we can provide for their business.

We will engage in direct marketing through the use of business cards. These cards will be issued to staff members to distribute to business owners who might benefit from our services. Because of the large number of businesses in the area, direct contact of our staff members with business owners will likely promote our business better and can be more attractive as it is a personal experience. The business cards will include our contact information as well as list our website for the customer to visit. Our motto will be clearly stated on the card "Our business is putting your company ahead of your competition."

We will be advertising our business in the local telephone books as well. We will place our advertisements under the accountants section to promote our tax preparation services, as well as under the business consultants section. These ads will include a list of our services, our contact number, and our website address. Through advertising in the telephone book, we hope to attract customers to our website, and eventually have them call our company.

ASFCN Consultants will also be sending out direct advertisements to local businesses. We will be developing flyers to send out to business owners. The flyers will be sent out at the beginning of each month to approximately 100 possible customers. The intention of spacing the mailings out is try to prevent overloading our staff with new customers in the event that there is a high response to our mailings. We will also engage in a second direct marketing program from January through April when we will send out direct mailings for our tax preparation services.

Finally, we will use social media to try to make contact with other small businesses in the area. The company will devise a Facebook page for our company to try to get the word out about our company. This is a great way to make connections with others in the area.

ASFCN Consultants will rely heavily on personal interaction with possible customers. Since we are a small business, we want to be able to provide our customers with competitive prices. To ensure this, we want to keep our marketing budget low, and instead focus on direct contact with potential customers. Direct marketing works most effectively when there is a connection that is made between business owners. It is believed that operating on a personal level with other businesses owners will help to further my own company.

IMC Budget

ASFCN Consultants prides ourselves on our ability to provide competitive rates to our customers. We recognize the significant amount of money that it costs to market a business, and because of this, we will be avoiding very general forms of mass marketing such as television, newspaper, and radio advertisements. Instead, we will be focusing on making direct connections with our possible customers. This is because there is no better way to attract customers than to reach out to them on a personal level and connect with them.

Engaging in direct marketing will require flyers and business cards to be developed. It is decided to use FedEx to print my flyers and my business cards alike. Using FedEx, flyers will cost me $599.99 for 2,500 flyers. Similarly, FedEx will charge $79.99 for 2,500 business cards. These will be of utmost importance to the marketing of my company as these will be either handed directly to business owners or mailed to them. Stamps and envelops are also going to be added in to the direct mailings. A coil of 3,000 stamps from the post office will be bought, which will cost the company $1,320. The envelopes for the business will cost $369.99 for 2,000 envelopes.

The first avenue for marketing will be setting up a website for my company. The design and layout will be of utmost importance to the success of this website. This will also be very important because all of the other avenues of advertising will promote the website for customers to visit for more information. It is important that the website is professional and provides customers with information on our mission, our staff, as well as detailed descriptions of our services. For website design, a 3rd party designer will be used. The cost of website design is estimated to be $650, with a $30 monthly web hosting fee.

Besides simply having a website, advertising via Facebook and Craigslist will be used.

The beauty is that both of these online communications platforms are free. On the Facebook page, staff members of ASFCN Consultants will be able to provide other businesses with basic business information and direct them to the company web site to learn more. Craigslist is much the same. It is a free site to offer services in the general area.

The company will also be advertising through Yellowpages.com. The price for this service is $41.00 a month and a print advertisement in the Yellow Pages will also be shown for $115. I will be advertising in the surrounding Yellow Page editions. Finally, some print ads will also be made in the Talking Phone Book. The cost is about $750.

When all is said and done, the total amount for advertising for the first year will be $4070.97. In our opinion, this is a feasible amount of money to be spending on advertising to get the company off and running. It is obvious that the price of advertising increases very quickly, especially when first starting out as a company. Advertising is a necessity to keeping a business running, and spending $4000 is a great investment into a successful business.

Conclusion

This marketing plan summarizes the Unique Selling Propositions of ASFCN Consultants and discusses how it intends to enter the market with a wide range of marketing activities. The plan projects a 3-year gross revenue of $228K. The cost structure is expected to be in-line with industry average. Marketing activities will mainly includes placing advertisements in the YellowPage and also making use of online social networking platforms such as Facebook.

Web Consulting Service

Highlights of this Marketing Plan:
1. Goals are shown early on in the plan
2. A short history about the industry is provided
3. Comprehensive competitive analysis

Executive Summary:

Social Media platforms have quickly become a crucial component of networking and marketing strategies for nearly any business that desires to be successful in this era. As a Social Media consultancy firm, ASFCN Web Consultants seeks to capitalize on the growing trend and utilization of Social Media's growing importance. We specialize in developing and deploying online Social Media campaigns that create social capital, brand awareness, and revenue generation. Our unique concept provides comprehension, design, implementation and sustainability of a business's comprehensive Social Media solutions to enable clients to Tweet, blog, post, publish, socialize, advertise, and market with optimal magnitude and scope via Social Media outlets. Our primary technical focus is to remain on the "cutting edge" of new technology. The added benefits to our clientele are multifaceted but have at their core the goal of any business: providing clients with what they want as efficiently as possible, and our goal is to align our customers with their specific consumer base.

Goals and Values:

Year 1:
- Conduct initial outreach to potential clients to spread awareness.

- Steadily increase advertisement-generated revenue for clients and foster quarterly growth while decreasing the clients' costs reassessing in-house technological usage.

Year 2-4:
- Evaluate attainment of past goals after performing quarterly evaluation(s) and implement any necessary changes and improvements reinvesting earnings in the business.

- Increase brand awareness and reputation by striving to provide consistent, superior, value-added services to clients reassessing in-house technological usage. Establish beneficial joint ventures and advantageous collaborative working relationships.

Year 5 – On:
- Re-evaluate attainment of past goals after performing quarterly evaluation(s) and implement any necessary changes and improvements. Reinvest our earnings in the business.

- Analyze progress and align business to best meet the specific needs and characteristics of our clients.

Mission Statement:

ASFCN Web Consultants combines the needs of the supplier with the demands of the consumer in a digital manner such that automation and proactive marketing exposure is benchmarked at a higher level. The purpose of ASFCN Web Consultants is to empower its clients with the capacity to integrate Social Media into networking and marketing strategies targeting online visibility. Our enterprise assists companies in viewing, comprehending and evaluating the benefits of Social Media as a potentially crucial addition.

Our mission is to achieve the best Social Media Optimization by maximizing the metrics used to assess the performance and quality. Our mission is to optimize each part and all resources used, whether human capital, hardware or software related. Some of the metrics employed to assess Social Media campaigns consist of:

- Media coverage
- Traffic / unique visitors
- Customer surveys and user ratings
- Automation and personalization
- Conversations (blogs, tweets, postings, etc.)
- Navigability
- Return visits and next clicks
- Keyword usage and density
- Retrieval rankings
- Inbound links
- Engagement duration
- Profits

The Current Market and Social Media Marketing:

Recently, there has been a significant shift in the way companies are choosing to engage their customer base, push advertisements and communicate updates. Traditional media outlets, such as magazines, newspapers and television, offer one-way information dissemination. However, the new model of brand promotion involves using Social Media sources to create a two-way dialog between companies and their customers. Current studies show that companies worldwide are seeking more effective ways to build a stronger and more loyal consumer base with a more targeted focus on consumer needs. Companies are also able to obtain information from a client instantly, which in turn provides useful data that can be used to improve prospective and current client experiences. At the same time, consumers are looking for companies to provide personalized, targeted and engaging services. The convergence of these two movements has created an interesting need for managing Social Media marketing in a way that meets the goals of both the company and the consumer. This need continues to grow as companies realize that while the Social Media explosion presents new benefits and opportunities, it also creates new challenges as they struggle to understand how this technology can and should be used.

Social Media refers to the web-based communication sources that foster interaction between the online communities. Social Networking sites such as Facebook, Twitter and LinkedIn are some of the more popular sources for connecting friends, family, businesses and professionals. On the other hand, Social Media Marketing is about targeting specific markets and developing conversations and relationships in places where those markets can actively communicate. Social Media marketing benefits the provider and the consumer. One of the greatest benefits of these sites is that both the supplier and the customer stop being mere "content absorbers" and instead become "content creators" by contributing to the marketplace, community and client / supply base their own thoughts and ideas. Companies are using Social Media to advance new relationships, increase audience reach with minimal expense, lower customer acquisition costs and deliver real-time updates. With the rise of Social Media usage, there is a growing business need around managing the Social Media effort for companies.

Historic Overview:
Historically, technology has changed too rapidly for the average company to keep up.

Predecessors to Social Media include:
- Usernets
- BBSs (Bulletin Board Systems)
- IRC
- ICQ and Instant Messaging

Some early social networks include:
- Dating sites
- Forums such as Six Degrees, AsianAvenue, MiGente, BlackPlanet, LiveJournal and World of Warcraft / MMORPGS

Major advances in social networking include:
- Friendster, Hi5, LinkedIn, MySpace and Facebook

- Media Sharing includes Photobucket, Flickr, YouTube, Revver, Delicious, Digg and Reddit
- Real time updates include Twitter, Posterous and Tumblr

Differentiator:

ASFCN Web Consultants combines the needs of the supplier with the demands of the consumer in a digital manner such that automation and proactive marketing exposure is benchmarked at a higher level. Our focus is to remain within the "cutting edge" so that the customers do not have to. The services we provide to our clients may be considered invaluable for achieving a magnitude of sustainability, a scope of productivity and a standard far better than the current marketplace.

Businesses are seeking ways to stay competitive in their markets that are cost efficient while increasing customer base and company productivity. Our services allow business owners to focus on the business. The aim to effectively meet the needs of the industries we serve is paramount. ASFCN Web Consultants will offer innovative new approaches to Social Media with multiple sites, concentrating on the most popular and successful: Facebook, LinkedIn and Twitter. We will also offer QQ (China) and Cyworld (Korea) to international clients. Another key difference is our focus on charitable giving and nonprofits.

Product or Service Description:

Our company will provide a Social Media consultancy service to clients enabling them to augment their traditional approaches with these new and often more efficient marketing strategies. ASFCN Web Consultants will be based in Manchester, NH, and some services may be virtual at a client's request.

Services Offered:

- Analysis of client's utilization of Social Media
- Design, writing, management and development of Social Media sites and events
- Origination and distribution of client related updates from news, blogs, postings, and tweets
- Search engine optimization, marketing and reputation management
- Sending birthday greetings
- Creating and augmenting online relationships
- Creating and maintaining progress reports
- Creating content ideas

SWOT Analysis:

Strengths:
- Creative, talented and proficient yet practical, quick, very accessible and effective service with In depth knowledge of and capacity to automate Social Media marketing and optimization campaigns and proficiency in financial management while allowing for charitable giving.
- ASFCN Web Consultants has the capability to drive our client's online content to help form active community relationships through low cost exposure and non-traditional messages with members providing full analysis of what is being reported about our clients.

Weaknesses:
- Social Media is new and our company will seem even newer. Some of our competitors have been providing this service for some time and as such, we may have a hard time developing brand awareness as a start up. The company currently possesses insufficient access to numerous resources available to our competitors with a limited operating history.
- There is also a lack of tools and / or resources to track and monitor campaign results and more potential for negative exposure, which could become time consuming.

Opportunities:
- ASFCN Web Consultants team members have all been participating within this growing industry before becoming involved in the company's actual start up. We can use our collective experience to reach many people at a very little cost and float new ideas before implementation.
- The growth in social networking, social shopping, blogging, etc. offers our targeted customers a method and means to attract consumers and build personal relationships. We can create promotions, discounts and offers that can be utilized through Social Media platforms.

Threats:
- We need to remain conscious of viruses, Malware and digital intrusion efforts and changes occurring at Third Party Service Providers such as web hosting, ISP suppliers and Social Networking Portals.
- Executives may not understand the mechanics and administrations of Social Media and may thus not perceive the value in our service. Some companies are

concerned that Social Media services may provide only a very limited personal touch.

Key Success Factors And / Or Major Pitfalls:

Key successes would include sound management practices, industry experience, technical support and planning ability. We will target the fact that we are a new company, which could be seen as a disadvantage for us. New should be exciting though and a company that people would want to check out. ASFCN Web Consultants will develop and grow a system, so all of our work is streamlined and perfected further and all decisions for the company will be well thought out. As the team is already focused on charitable giving, we should avoid the issue that too many start-ups have of being too focused on personal wealth too quickly. The success of a Social Media marketing and optimization program depends on the following factors: transparency, honesty, relevance, value and growth. ASFCN Web Consultants will assist companies with their image, investor / media / customer relations, sales and internal communications.

ASFCN Web Consultants will work hard to be realistic about our workload, and will form connections and network in such a way to consistently have projects for the team and to hopefully have a support system. We will work hard to provide excellent customer satisfaction, which will hopefully lead to repeated business from existing clientele and new client acquisition through current client references. Similarly, we hope to avoid poor customer satisfaction, which would lead to no repeated business from existing clients and no new clients acquisition. We will also try to avoid over depending on a single individual or on a predicted specific event.

Target Market:

Target Population:

The target marketplace includes individuals, businesses and entities demanding a modern Internet presence for networking and marketing purposes. Total target population is yet to be determined. Client demographic ratios will be equally male / female. Most of our clients and their audiences will be technology savvy, which is to say that they will at least have access to computers and the Internet.

Charitable Giving:

Once the company is self-supporting, ASFCN Web Consultants will also reach out to the non-profit sector, with a goal of making this 20% of the overall services at no or little cost to eligible 501C(3)s each year. Upon building a solid clients base and credibility, ASFCN Web Consultants will move on to establish specific applications and guidelines for serving those non-profits who have the best models for serving their target populations.

What information is the target audience searching for?

The target audience is searching for particular companies and products. It is our responsibility to create a message that will fully capture their attention and make them interested in taking action. In today's economic climate, most consumers are affected more by their peers' recommendations and lower prices than by brand loyalty because there is virtually no limit to the access consumers have to each brand offering the same product.

Competitive Analysis:

ASFCN Web Consultants will face two types of competitors: traditional marketing and other interactive marketing Social Media companies. For competitors, a variety of domestic companies that specialize in Social Media marketing were considered.

Company / Service	ABC Web	DEF Social Media Inc.	GHI Group	Team JKL!	MNO Group	PQR Ltd.	ASFCN Web Consultants
Leadership and Management:	X	-	X	X	-	-	X
Strategy:	X	X	X	-	-	X	X
Innovation, Implementation and Design:	X	X	X	X	-	X	X
Research and Monitoring:	-	X	X	X	-	X	X
Word Of Mouth Marketing:	-	-	-	X	X	-	X
Social Applications Development:	-	-	-	X	-	-	X
Public Relations:	X	X	X	X	X	X	X
Social Media Optimization:	-	-	-	-	X	X	X
Influencer Marketing:	-	-	-	-	X	-	X

Competitive Analysis (Service)

Company / Differentiator	ABC Web	DEF Social Media Inc.	GHI Group	Team JKL!	MNO Group	PQR Ltd.	ASFCN Web Consultants
Thought Leadership:	X	X	X	X	X	X	X
Research:	X	X	X	X	-	X	X
Consulting:	X	-	X	X	X	X	X
Art, Science and Practical Application Of Social:	-	X	X	-	-	X	X
"The Original Social Media Agency":	-	-	-	X	-	-	-
Full Service Advertising:	-	-	-	-	X	X	-
"New Media Agency of the Year" - The Holmes Report:	-	-	-	-	X	X	-

Competitive Analysis (Differentiator)

Financial Analysis:

Breakeven Analysis:

Fixed Costs per Month
Rent $500.00
Phone/Internet $60.00
Insurance $100.00
Other fixed costs $5000.00
Total Fixed Cost   **$5660.00**

1 Unit = 1 hour consulting
1 Hour Service Fee = $100.00
Variable costs = $30.00 per hour; Contribution Margin = $100.00 - $30.00 = $70.00
Total Monthly Costs = $5660
Monthly breakeven = $5660 / 70 ≈ 80 hours

Since the average number of chargeable consulting hours is expected to be at the 140 to 150 per month, this business will be a profitable one because the break-even requirement is 80 hours.

Product Pricing Structure:

Our pricing will be reflected of our competitors who work with small and mid size companies until we are able to take on larger clients. When determining the price per client, there are several factors we plan to consider: the size of clients, how evolved they are in their understanding of Social Media and their goals and objectives. In addition, training and updates (content wise) will be per hour (especially for customization) roughly at $100 / hour depending on the client.

Our prices will be indicative of the fact that we are a new company attempting to survive while creating maximum profit and market share. We understand that the demand for our services is dependant upon educating our clients about the need for our service. Costs to the company will be very minimal at about $30, as we provide a service to companies and not a physical good. Our employees can work virtually as long as they have access to the Internet and phone services. The customer segment will affect our pricing as larger companies can pay more than medium and small sized companies. Eventually, once ASFCN Web Consultants grows and expands we will utilize premium pricing once our reputation has been established. Some of our clients will be high value deal stickers as they are looking to save the most for their budgets and as such perceive Social Media to be a great alternative to traditional marketing, which frequently is more expensive. Our customers will also be a wide combination of service / quality, price / value and affinity customers.

Channels of Distribution:

ASFCN Web Consultants will be based in New York, NY. Some services may be carried out virtually at a client's request. For our physical location, we will have a beautiful office where we can meet with our local clients or those who choose to travel or those whom we invite. We will also hire employees in accordance with the amount of projects we have. We will work hard to monitor customer satisfaction through having great staff members. We will consider the possibility of hiring part time employees, contractors and interns while deciding on our clients and how many we are hoping to serve. To save costs, we will also consider the idea of sharing an office with a different business or having a virtual office space.

Our company will be pure service focusing on the process and will serve a business need providing Social Media services. The objective will be profit and we will focus on search, experience and credence qualities. ASFCN Web Consultants will work hard so that our customers can see the value before, during and after the service has been completed. We will have product variety with the sites we utilize and upon the preference of customization for our clients. Our company will have expert power, as we will provide knowledge of Social Media, which will be different from the traditional media. We will also create a value network where we will set partnerships and alliances with other marketing agencies that offer graphic design, copy writing, etc. services such that we could refer businesses to one another.

Our sales representatives will mostly serve for deliveries, missionaries and educating our clients about the need for Social Media. We are hoping to empower our customers through educating about their basic Social Media needs. We will also work on co-production. They will also be solution providers solving problems for our clients. Our sales force will prospect, target, communicate, sell and service. Our technological team will have the opportunity to work as a contractual sales force commission based dependent upon the amount of sales. In this way, the team who produces the actual services to our clients will also sell the services simultaneously saving costs. ASFCN Web Consultants will utilize both the push and pull promotional strategies. Our clients will ask for our services, however, we will also educate them on the crucial need for them. Our sales team will also act as demand creators finding creative approaches to sell Social Media services. We will also allow for benefits (35%) for sales personnel, which could already be included as our technical team serves in the sales role.

Integrated Marketing Communication (IMC):

Our growth model consists of starting with small companies and organizations, developing credibility in the business community and expanding towards larger organizations. A message that is sent to our stakeholders and our primary objective for our promotional approach will be focused on our mission statement of the fact that we provide a variety of Social Media services while focusing on charitable giving. ASFCN Web Consultants will build business-to-business relationships with companies who may offer services to other businesses or consumers. Our hope is that potential clients and leads will come to the company rather than having to market ourselves and taking a hard sell approach. Initially, the Internet through SMO (Social Media Optimization) and SEO (Search Engine Optimization) techniques will give ASFCN Web Consultants a broad reach and unlimited potential clients. As some of our target market might consist of individuals who are not media savvy themselves, we also plan to attend face-to-face networking events.

IMC Budget:

The first year will be focused on the Social Media outreach and attending networking events. ASFCN Web Consultants team members have all been participating within this growing industry before becoming involved in the company's actual start up. We can use our collective experience to reach many people at a very little cost and float new ideas before implementation. The costs associated with attending networking events vary geographically. Most events around New York, NY are about $0-50 per event, so the average would be $25. If one member of our staff attends one event a week:

$$\$25 * 4.5 \text{ weeks} * 12 \text{ months} = \$1350$$

Our technological team will have the opportunity to work as a contractual sales force commission based depending on the amount of sales. We also need to remember to include benefits (35%) for sales personnel, again this amount will depend on how many clients we have. Our sales force will prospect, target, communicate, sell and service.

We will not spend money on promoting on the radio, print publications, etc. until our business grows and we have the finances we can implement for this. When surveying personal connections, these are the numbers we are considering if we implement print media in the future:

- Newspaper - $1,300 (Weekly rate for a 2 inch by 2 inch Ad)
- Direct Mail - $1,500 (Rate for 1,000 4 inch by 6 inch Postcards)
- Radio - $100 per spot

Conclusion:

Social networking platforms such as Facebook and MySpace have become the new "Meeting Places" for many people. It is no longer an online avenue for people to post photos or exchange greeting notes. More and more businesses, especially the small-to-medium sized ones, are taking advantage of this fast growing online platform to communicate with their potential and existing customers. ASFCN Web Consultants is determined to enter the market with its industry knowledge and hands-on expertise in social networking. Service will be charged at $100 per hour with a monthly break-even point at 80 hours which is feasible from the management team's perspective. Marketing activities will be limited to attending local networking events to promote the service.

Chapter 7 – Marketing Plan Example – Business Products

Highlights of this Marketing Plan:
1. Problems of competitor's products are shown to help the justification of the proposed product
2. Good discussion of target market using segmentation
3. Good financials

Executive Summary

ASFCN Software Inc. is a telecommunications engineering design tool software developer. ASFCN Software Inc. will introduce an engineering design tool called ASFCN-Now that network engineers working for telecommunications carriers as well as network engineers working for engineering services providers can access via their corporate intranet through a web-browser of the companies choice. The beauty of this tool is that it will not require expensive investments in proprietary software bundles or packages as it is built on SQL programming language and allows for a web-browsing-like interface on company servers. This simple design does not require significant server memory to operate and is highly scalable and customizable given the nature of the SQL language.

Product Description

The product that we, ASFCN Software Inc., will bring to market is a web-browser based engineering design tool called, ASFCN-Now that will be used by engineers working within the wireless and wire line telecommunication, carrier field as well as by engineering vendors providing engineering services for telecommunications carries.

The tool will be used mainly to develop site-specific, detailed installation specifications used by installers of telecommunications and other communications network hardware and equipment. The system will allow engineers throughout the industry to produce standardized installation specifications as outlined by Telcordia in their industry standard document GR-1502-CORE.

The *problem* that many telecommunications engineers employed by network carriers face is outsourcing of engineering services where EF&I (Engineering, Furnish & Install) vendors do the actual detail engineering and create installation specifications to be used by network installation teams to follow. This can often result in a reduction of the number of engineers employed by carriers (i.e., downsizing), as well as a general loss of detail engineering knowledge to outside vendors. This product will allow for telecommunications engineering to remain in-house as the design will allow for ease-of-use as well as efficient production of quality, installation specifications that can be used throughout the industry at large. Retaining engineering services in-house can increase employee knowledge of network engineering as well as eliminate expenditures for vendor engineering services. For those carriers who do not wish to return to or retain in-house engineering, this product can also be marketed to engineering service firms interested in streamlining and standardizing the detailed installation specification process.

The system will allow for knowledge sharing amongst work teams as well as a training tool for entry-level engineers as specific job-type templates can be created, outlining required materials as well as basic work steps thereby eliminating hours of research by each engineer.

Following are a few examples of the product:

(Screenshot intentionally removed)

Notice above that specific technologies or network equipment specific templates can be built into the user interface by selected users (lead Engineers for example) to allow for consistent network installations.

(Screenshot 2 intentionally removed)

Above is a copy of the detailed work item input page where engineers add site-specific installation work items to the technology specific templates.

These are small examples of the robust functionality of ASFCN-Now in facilitating streamlined, consistent detailed installation specification output.

SWOT Analysis

Strengths

- Extensive industry knowledge and experience both working as telecommunications carrier detail engineers as well as working with and reviewing detail engineering work provided by EF&I vendors.
- Knowledge of communications carrier process flows and specific requirements.
- Software development process knowledge and experience with design of web-based knowledge sharing systems
- Understanding of the Business buying cycle and budgeting to capture market interest

Weaknesses

- Ability to secure capital necessary for initial design as well as future system enhancements
- Ability to attract and retain additional software engineers required for future releases
- Delivery of the product in time to meet critical buying cycle budgets, especially the timeliness of future software releases

Opportunities

- Broadband services revenues are expected to grow 62% for wireless carriers and at least 6% for wire-line carriers by 2015.
- Converging network trends will require increased investment in new hardware elements as well as removals of obsolete equipment from existing networks
- Offer a highly customizable solution to fit unique telecomm, or EF&I vendor engineering needs as well as to expand into the enterprise IT market

Threats

- Microsoft Office products, specifically excel, that many telecomm and EF&I Vendors currently utilize to create installation specification packages
- General economic downturn could force continued cost control measures for providers despite the anticipated broadband services revenues increase for both wireless and wire-line service companies

- Increased regulation and "net-neutrality" enforcement on broadband services that may force additional cost-cutting measures on network build out projects
- Increased competition from major software development companies already offering accounting and/or supply chain systems for telecomm and engineering vendor firms that could decide to incorporate a specification design tool module into existing systems

Target Markets

ASFCN Software Inc. understands the requirements of the network equipment expansion market and will utilize this understanding to better serve the needs of specific service provider and engineering services provider markets and develop our communications aimed at attracting these markets. Out initial target markets will include the following:

- Wireless Telecommunications service providers
- Wire-line Telecommunications service providers
- Telecommunications and network equipment Engineering, Furnish and Installation service providers (EF&I Vendors)

The profiles of the target ASFCN Software Inc. business consumers include the following:

- Geographic:

While ASFCN Software Inc. will initially role out our specification design software to our targeted business consumers in Canada and the USA, there is no limitation to international uses or sales. In fact, for those domestic service/services providers with current or anticipated international operations, the software can be customized to include and serve these international markets.

- Demographic:

The network equipment installation specification market segment can be defined as a niche business market as their needs are unique and clearly identifiable within the market segment.

ASFCN-Now will serve the specific needs of network design engineers working for telecommunications service providers as well as EF&I firms performing engineering services for telecommunications providers. Our understanding of the very specific input and output needs of this segment make this target market attractive to our current and future plans for the development of our ASFCN-Now software.

Behavioral Segmentation (the B2B Buying Decision):

As ASFCN-Now was developed for use by the business market segments identified above, ASFCN Software Inc. will focus sales on our understanding of the business-to-business (B2B) buying cycle decision process flow we describe as follows:

- Identify the problem
- Create criteria
- Search for providers
- Evaluate options
- Test the solution
- Procure the solution

Our offering of ASFCN-Now to our selected target markets will center upon the first step in the B2B cycle, that is, at the point where decision makers first identify their business or efficiency problem. It will be our goal to assist the market decision makers in identifying the problem that they may not yet be aware even exists. The cost savings associated with the use of our product for carriers who currently outsource engineering services to EF&I vendors as well as the cost savings in terms of efficiency for those same EF&I vendors will highlight the unnecessary costs problem they already have. The identification of a cost problem can help business decision makers allocate or obtain a budget for our professional services product.

Market Trend and Growth:

Overall telecommunications services revenues are expected to grow at a rate of nearly 13.8 percent over the next few years, reaching $3.7 trillion by 2015. Anticipated Wireless services revenue growth leads the overall market while wireline services revenue follows in second place. For both markets, the revenues increases are expected to result from broadband services which will require continued provider investment in broadband services network equipment.

In fact, despite the general economic downturn of recent years, the telecommunications industry continues and is expected to continue growth at the double-digit percentage rate of 13.8% as economists see telecommunications as a key industry for increasing economic growth itself.

Current trends in Carrier Ethernet services such as metro-area and wide-area Ethernet services indicate that the market is expected to grow at a compounded rate of over 25 percent, increasing from $2.4 billion in 2009 to reach nearly $7.8 billion by 2014.

The above market trends will require continued upgrades of existing network equipment as well as continued installations of new network equipment by telecommunications carriers to deliver new services technologies.

Competitive Analysis

Although we consider ASFCN-Now as a program unique to and designed specifically for our selected market segments, we do realize that potential competition exists in the market. Our research into the existing products in use by our target markets revealed that a majority of carriers currently use Microsoft office products including Word or Excel to develop network equipment installation specifications.

The majorities (80%) of telecommunications providers that use in-house network engineers utilize "home-grown" Excel workbook templates with often complicated macros and linked formula cell formatting to produce specifications. We found the same to be true for the EF&I market although they tend to have more fully developed Excel templates accessible via servers which allows for minimal output standards and control.

The remaining (20%) of providers currently use systems developed by in-house IT employees. These systems are typically grown or added as modules to existing project tracking software that offer limited flexibility in terms of detailed equipment installation design parameters. Despite the substitute products identified above, ASFCN Software Inc. could eventually face direct competition by the following two (2) potential competitors:

ABC Solutions: A privately-held software solutions company dedicated to developing Bill of Materials (BOM) and Engineering Change Order (ECO) software that allows for collaboration, and up-to-date tracking information among work-teams.

- Current market is manufacturing companies providing product development tracking and collaboration software. Potential exists to enter our niche market by modifying their software to include network equipment installation specification output.

- No evidence exists that ABC Solutions has any penetration in our selected market segment, but the potential exists given their current product

- ABC Solutions currently serves 50,000 mid to small sized manufacturing companies worldwide.

- Current customers include Sierra Wireless, and Silver Spring Networks indicating their interest in wireless an networking markets

- Over $35 million in funding from investors such as Scale Venture Partners, and Greyhawk Capital Management

- Current product pricing is an average of $99.00 per user, per month. $99.00 is the starting price that increases based on level(s) of customization and support.

CDE SOLUTIONS: Produced and owned by the not-for-profit organization, Construction Sciences Research Foundation (CSRF), CDE SOLUTIONS is a database of pre-written full-length, short-form and outline master guide specification Sections designed to be used for preparation of project specifications and to create a company master specification system.

- Current markets do include engineering and electrical construction specification users.

- CDE SOLUTIONS uses a word-processing based edit-and-delete process that accommodates a wide range of projects, from those where only simple edits are required, to those where extensive customizing is needed.

- CDE SOLUTIONS uses Microsoft Word to provide specification development utilized by those responsible for preparing specifications.

- Again, no evidence exists that CDE SOLUTIONS has any share of our current target markets, but there is potential for their entrance to the Telcordia standard network equipment installation specification market as the CSRF is dedicated to providing common language services for the construction specification fields as Telcordia general requirements do for network installation fields.

- Pricing for CDE SOLUTIONS is listed per specification section. Each section is a sub-set of the master library for a given discipline like electrical engineering for example. Each library is broken down into sections of installation requirements and is priced at $115 per section, per user, for this first year with an annual renewal fee of $90.00 each year.

While each of the above products could potentially evolve to become direct competition for ASFCN-Now, our product is designed specifically for the network equipment installation market and as such is tailored to meet the unique needs of those markets in their adherence to the general Telcordia standards outlined solely for their industry in GR-1502-CORE. Further, our product can be customized to meet the specific needs of each service provider in our target markets and can be further modified to incorporate emerging technologies equipment installation requirements. The consumer can do these modifications as the software allows users to create equipment specific templates that can be shared by all local users. Some additional features that provide points-of-differentiation for ASFCN-Now include:

- Server based, intranet access through web-browser to our program allows for controlled usage

- No uncontrolled, complicated macro development required as would be for template designed using Microsoft office products such as Excel.

- Enables equipment engineering knowledge sharing as equipment specific installation templates can be developed and shared.

- Facilitates consistency in technology deployment across geographic footprints through use of design templates

- Streamlines Bill of Materials creation to materials procurement process as BOMs can be exported to logistics/supply chain software

- System functionality facilitates training for entry-level network engineers as common/ best practices steps can be customized into specification creation process

Financial Analysis

The following financial analysis is based on the telecommunications market growth trends identified above and is the result of ASFCN Software Inc.'s anticipated market share growth strategy. We believe that these forecasts are conservative and we expect to attain at least these levels of financial success.

The Break-Even analysis was calculated based on annual sales rather than monthly to account for monthly variations in the telecommunications business buying cycle and quarterly expense budget allocations for software investments in line with overall telecom network investment spending.

To break-even, ASFCN Software will have to sell 1514 licenses annually to earn sales revenue equal to $134,753.

Break Even Analysis Data:

Annual Units to Break-Even	1514
Annual Sales to Break-Even	$134,753

Assumptions:

Average Per-Unit Revenue	$89.00
Average Per-Unit Variable Cost	$18.00
Estimated Annual Fixed Cost	$107,500 ($8,958 Monthly)

The following three year sales forecast is based on our currently proposed product license pricing and support services which will remain constant over the forecasted period as part of our strategy to keep pricing 10% below existing competition pricing, despite the fact that we believe our product is unique to our target market and will face minimal direct competition.

Sales Forecast			
Sales	**2011**	**2012**	**2013**
Telco Carriers	$ 73,425	$ 78,142	$ 97,900
EF&I Vendors	$ 81,702	$ 88,021	$ 106,800
Total Sales	**$ 155,127**	**$ 166,163**	**$ 204,700**

Sales Forecast

The above forecast assumes that the industry growth rates identified above in the market trend and growth section will continue as predicted. The assumed sales growth rate is averaged out to be approximately 13% over the three-year period as telecommunications carriers/service providers continue to invest in new network technologies over these same years. For year three, 2013, the additional increase is expected as increased industry awareness of our product will enable additional sales.

Sensitivity Analysis:

Although we conclude that the above sales forecast is conservative at the average sales increase of 13% over the three year term given the current market industry growth expectations (25% as documented above), we have calculated a worst-case analysis below to account for possible unexpected downturns in carrier network investment.

The above forecast assumes only a 10% increase in sales over the three-year period. In this scenario, the revenues do exceed the break-even amount if 134,753 in year one (2011) and continue to increase approximately 10% each year thereafter.

Product Pricing Structure

We have developed our pricing structure to gain *maximum market share* by setting our product price to an average of $89 per user license. This introductory price is %10 lower than the average of our competitors' product pricing. With our market penetration strategy, we expect to gain favorable market-share not only by setting our initial price lower than our existing competitors, but to continue the lower pricing to create a perceived barrier of entry to this market from potential future competition. We intend to continue this maximum market share pricing strategy by continually monitoring costs, both variable per-unit and fixed, while increasing sales and future product enhancements.

Our price of $89 per user license will also facilitate our customer's perceived value of our product offering as our intent is to continue to offer low-cost software enhancements as well as continued support for these products to achieve quality brand-recognition. Our understanding of recent trends by telecommunications carriers to implement process reengineering to reduce overall costs allowed us to price ASFCN-Now strategically to align with the overall efficiency goals of our customer market.

Again, we document our Price and Cost structure below:

Average Per-Unit Revenue	$89.00
Average Per-Unit Variable Cost	$18.00
Estimated Annual Fixed Cost	$107,500 ($8,958 Monthly)

We used the above figures to display our following three year projected Revenue and Profitability forecasts based on our current pricing startegy for both of our target markets:

Revenue & Profitability

	Year 1	Year 2	Year 3
Unit Sales			
Telco Carriers	825	878	1100
EF&I Vendors	918	989	1200
Total Unit Sales	1743	1867	2300
Sales			
Telco Carriers	$ 73,425.00	$ 78,142.00	$ 97,900.00
EF&I Vendors	$ 81,702.00	$ 88,021.00	$ 106,800.00
Total Sales (Revenue)	**$ 155,127.00**	**$ 166,163.00**	**$ 204,700.00**
Direct Unit Costs			
Telco Carriers	$ 18.00	$ 18.00	$ 18.00
EF&I Vendors	$ 18.00	$ 18.00	$ 18.00
Direct Cost of Sales			
Telco Carriers	$ 14,850.00	$ 15,804.00	$ 19,800.00
EF&I Vendors	$ 16,524.00	$ 17,802.00	$ 21,600.00
Subtotal Direct Cost of Sales	**$ 31,374.00**	**$ 33,606.00**	**$ 41,400.00**
Contribution Margin			
Telco Carriers	$ 58,575.00	$ 62,338.00	$ 78,100.00
EF&I Vendors	$ 65,178.00	$ 70,219.00	$ 85,200.00
Total contribution Margin	$ 123,753.00	$ 132,557.00	$ 163,300.00
Profit			
Total Profit	**$ 16,253.00**	**$ 25,057.00**	**$ 55,800.00**

Revenue and Profitability

Channels of Distribution

Because it is part of ASFCN Software Inc.'s strategy to establish, evolve and maintain valuable relationships with our customers, we intend to provide direct sales to our target markets for the foreseeable future. Our initial investment in materials required for distributing our software product will be limited to writable CDs and minimal packaging materials for those customers who prefer installing the software on their servers directly as opposed to remote software downloads from our server.

For shipping any requested user manuals, ASFCN Software Inc., will utilize USPS, FedEx or UPS depending on the address and required timeliness of the delivery. As we grow over the first few years, we do not anticipate requiring and established or contractual relationship with a specific distribution partner.

Our primary method of distribution will be onsite delivery and installation as the work required is minimal and can be done within a matter of a few hours. This method is in line with our overarching strategy to provide personalized support whereby we can display our knowledge of the specific requirements of the telecommunications industry. We assume that this will further our word-of-mouth sale leads.

Integrated Marketing Communication and Budget

Our strategy for marketing ASFCN-Now will be focused directly on our knowledge of the industry requirements as well as on the cost savings our product will provide in terms of time and labor efficiency as well as in terms of network design knowledge retention.

We will launch ads in Industry-specific publications including both print magazine media as well as online advertising on industry-specific websites. Our selected websites are those that are owned and run by the same companies that publish the printed magazines as our strategy includes purchasing advertising *packages* that include both printed as well as online ads to save on incremental advertising costs.

Our secondary, although equally significant promotional effort will include attending industry trade and technology forums where we can display ASFCN-Now and allow consumers the opportunity to use the product as well as review various samples of printed Detailed Installation Specifications.

Our third promotional strategy will be to contact industry leaders directly and offer onsite demonstrations of ASFCN-Now. This strategy is dependent on our direct industry experience and valuable networks of industry leader contacts as well. Our plans for onsite product demonstrations center on gathering not only leaders and management, but displaying the usability to the knowledge workers and engineers who can place upward pressure or suggestion to budget the purchase of ASFCN-Now in time for the next buying cycle.

Our promotional activities include:
- Monthly ½ page horizontal ads in both OSP Magazine and Telecommunications Magazine
- Annual advertisement on both OSP and Telecommunications online websites as a featured site sponsor which secures a position at the top middle of the website:
- Sponsorship advertisement includes:
- 468 x 60 pixel top banner
- ad position as top center of page below publication banner
- three micro banners, (88 x 31 pixels each)

- Integrated communications package from Network World Publications including both ½ page print ad, website banner ad, as well as featured vendor at select telecommunications network engineering events.

The following shows the first year Integrated Marketing Budget allocations:

Marketing Expense Budget

Industry Magazine Publications	$13,516.00
Industry Specific Website Ads	$4,600.00
Industry Trade/Tech Forums	$23,000.00
Other media (brochures/flyers)	$3,000.00
Total Sales and Marketing Expenses	$44,116.00

Conclusion

The proposed engineering design software tool, ASFCN-Now, is going to bring ASFCN Software Inc. a 3-year profitabiOther media (brochures/flyers)
$3,000.00 lity of $97K. This is a strategic product to be launched because the market currently demands such a solution and our competitors' offerings are not that competitive. The sales and marketing expenses are expected to total $44K in the first year of launch, with the majority of spending on industrial magazine and trade show advertising.

High Technology Manufacturing (Telecom)

Highlights of this Marketing Plan:
1. Product is well described
2. Expected industry response is discussed
3. A sample press release is included

Executive Summary

ASFCN Manufacturing Inc. provides the technical competence and range to deliver global system solutions. From conception through design, we provide the manufacturing, integration, logistics, and deployment of custom solutions. Our global aspect provides a neighborhood presence in the crucial technology markets.

ASFCN Manufacturing is a business unit of ASFCN Technology Inc. The company specializes in turnkey system solutions for the communications, computer, and networking industries. We offer full-service design, manufacturing, integration, logistics, and deployment capacity. We work in concert with our Local, Regional, and Global OEM's, Service Providers, and Program Management Customers to facilitate designs that are tailored to their needs. We provide flexible production capabilities designed to meet customer's ever-changing delivery needs. Part of our solution means working with customers to expedite a new service or product to market. Our customers come first, and we prove this through facility flexibility, cutting-edge designs, and turn-around times.

The current cell site market is composed of Heavy Weight Concrete Shelters (60%), Light Weight Shelters (30%), and Metal Cabinet Enclosures (10%). Our goal is to eventually replace both the Heavy Weight Shelters, and the Light Weight Shelters, representing 90% of the Cell Sites out there. This number would equate to 15,458 cell sites per year. This represents a $433 million dollar product opportunity with a price tag of $28,000.00 per unit for the Global2000 Shelter. Revenue for equipment installation, integration, as well as unit installation and commissioning has not been included in this projection.

We expect Global2000 to be well received because of the difficulty in obtaining land for cell sites. We also expect customers will embrace this concept because of its ease of deployment. Our sales projections for Global2000 will be 10% market share per year for the first three years. In round numbers, first year – 1718 Global2000 Shelters; $4.81 million, second year – 3435 Global2000 shelters; $9.62 million, and the third year – 5153 Global2000 Shelters; $14.43 million.

Product Description

Global2000 is an innovative base station that provides the capability of a cabinet and the operational performance of a shelter. Shelters have become the predominate choice for Service Providers as they are easy to build, very strong, and cost effective systems that provide environmental protection for both technicians and equipment. The downside to shelters is that they are heavy.

There is a growing reliance on equipment cabinets, as they are smaller in size and provide a much lighter alternative to shelters. With the increase in zoning laws and the additional limits placed on land use, the access and choice of useable property has gotten to be very limited. To add to the problem, wireless networks continue to grow with the introduction of new and emerging technology. This lack of usable property has created yet a new bandwidth restriction that could threaten to put a halt to deployment of the latest technologies.

Raw land sites able to handle both single and multiple carriers must be utilized more fully. The smaller and less accessible sites are being considered as potential site candidates. Rooftops, raised structures, and tenant improvements have become more popular options for network expansion. As such, compact and light-weight metal shelters have become the required solution for cell site deployment. With the increase in network density, cabinets have become the obvious choice for cell sites. In addition, the pace of network additions and expansion and expansion has generated logistical opportunities for the more efficient storage, delivery, and handling features that a compact and lightweight enclosure provides.

OEM's have begun integration of these base stations into outdoor enclosures that provide for quicker deployment from the factory to installation site than what was previously seen with site integration of these units. Cabinets due lack the load-carrying capacity, equipment flexibility, and the protection from the elements that a shelter provides. These shortcomings are due in part to the design characteristics that provide for their light-weight and compactness.

Global2000 solves this dilemma and provides a new standard. A new standard that affords a complete solution that speaks to all the current challenges of base station deployment. Global2000 will present the smallest effective size possible for an enclosure of its kind. It provides the most efficient utilization of space without impact to operation or access to the equipment systems.

Global2000 will weigh between 10,000 to 15,000 pounds after full integration. A heavy weight shelter will weigh between 20,000 to 40,000 pounds without equipment. A light-weight shelter will weigh between 8,000 to 20,000 pounds without equipment. This is a significant weight advantage over shelters, with the advantage of being able to handle, transport, and site install this unit. Global2000 can be slung from its base with channels running across the width. The unit incorporates lateral resistance during handling through a floating spreader bar incorporated into its roof structure.

Global2000 will meet all common building code requirements for structural design. It will also meet 150 mph wind loading, Exposure C, and Seismic Zone IV requirements. Global2000 will afford the environmental protection of a walk-in shelter. It provides weather protection for equipment and personnel, and has single access door for service. The Global2000 unit has a dual stage air conditioning unit that can be tuned to provide optimal distribution throughout the unit.

Global2000 can support both racked and outdoor equipment. OEM equipment frames can be directly installed or their equipment can be reintegrated into high efficiency super frames. The interior equipment fixtures provide for flexible technology support, and allow for quick integration and dependable operation.

The Global2000 design specification is all about reduction and simplification of necessary mechanical operation. Each mechanical component was specified with a high degree of durability.

The key to Global2000's optimization of both design and operational effectiveness is in the equipment installation, deployment, and integration of design into a customer's network. The turnkey services provided by ASFCN leverage our technical expertise in coordination with our flexible manufacturing and global deployment capabilities under a single roof. Our business model assures that the communication, planning, execution, and accountability need to provide both speed of deployment and risk management in today's wireless landscape is assured.

Our production site is located in New York, NY. We are located in the heart of the Research Park with access to a major airport, major highways, and several major universities. We are also located approximately two hours from a major seaport.

Situational Analysis

Strengths:

- The Global2000 shelter design offers the wireless industry a space-efficient base station, designed for rapid, cost-effective deployment.

- The Global2000 has a small footprint, similar to a modular cabinet, yet offers the room of a walk-in shelter.

- The Global2000 provides room for expansion to meet market demands. Adding capacity, power, or ancillary equipment can be done without interruption to existing service.

- The Global2000 can be fully integrated and tested prior to reaching the installation site, which provides for a site ready solution when it leaves the production facility.

- The Global2000 can be staged at one of ASFCN many forward located staging facilities to help facilitate customer needs.

- The Global2000's lightweight, compact enclosure can easily be set in pace fully loaded, ready for utility hook-up and antenna connections.

- Lifting the unit can be accomplished by crane or helicopter for ground level or rooftop installation. Installation is complete with Commercial power, Antennas, and Telco lines.

- This quick installation allows your unit to be up and running, generating revenue before the last anchor bolt is secured.

Weaknesses:

- New design, although more cost effective than other shelters, customers may not embrace, as it is something new.

- Demand may exceed production capacity. Additional challenges can come from limited production due to learning curve due to a spike in initial demand.

- Supplier of shelter walls is a sole source vendor. Walls consist of foamed in place urethane insulation sandwiched between the interior and exterior metal surface.

- Wall design is proprietary, so vendor is also subject to delivery issues with his suppliers.

- Design is contingent upon Air Conditioning supplier coming up with a 2-stage, 8-ton air conditioning system to meet the shelter specifications we have proposed.

- Planning may be a challenge as this is a new product, forecasting of materials may not be accurate.

- Field support of these units will require learning curve time, and replacement parts may be a challenge initially.

Opportunities:

- This is a new market, potential could be huge.

- Expansion capabilities much greater with this system as is allows for scalability, giving your customer the opportunity for efficient expansion in a smaller space.

- Market niche that competitors have not been able to fill.

- Reduced customer site acquisition and maintenance costs as a result of Global2000's smaller overall footprint.

- Increased expansion capabilities allow your customer to keep his customers happy avoiding those dreaded dropped calls.

- Increased customer good will with a product that reduces overall customer cost by increasing cell subscriber coverage and reducing the number of new cell sites required.

- Global2000 allows inclusion of multiple customer technologies in the same shelter, thereby increasing customer capacity at a reduced cost.

Threats:

- Recession in the economy as we saw in 2001 which greatly impacted the cellular telephone market.

- Difficulty with various state regulating agencies as this unit is considered a habitable structure and must meet local building code requirements.

- Competitors could come up with a similar design, thereby impacting our market share.

- Customers not paying their bills, negatively impacting our ability to procure materials for additional shelter opportunities.

- Local governments may decide our shelter design is taxable, thereby creating additional financial burden.

- Inability to deliver production on time due to transportation challenges such as mechanical breakdowns.

Target Market

Our target market is going to consist of wireless carriers like Sprint, Verizon, and T-mobile. We will also be targeting OEMs. We will pursue emerging technology companies who are in the process of developing 4G technologies, as well as LTE, IEEE 802.11, and IEEE 802.16e. In addition, we will be targeting Program Management companies like NSORO, Bechtel, and Goodman. Finally, we will also be targeting Tower companies like ABC Corporation and CDE Corporation. Each of these companies represents a business market with significant potential. Each of the customers listed above represent our typical market. We provide wireless base stations to business customers. Our product is not a consumer purchased product.

Competitive Analysis

The two primary competitors are ABC Corporation of Chicago, IL, and CDE Corporation of Los Angeles, CA. The justification for selection of these two vendors was based on the current cell site composition in the United States. Site composition is 60% heavy weight (concrete) shelters, 30% light weight shelters, and 10% cabinets. New cell site construction is projected at 17,175 sites per year. These numbers are based on historical analysis obtained from CTIA's average installation for the past 10 years. CTIA – The Wireless Association is an international nonprofit organization founded in 1984, which represents all sectors of wireless communications. Both ABC Corp. and CDE Corp. produce heavy weight concrete shelters. These shelters along with lightweight concrete shelters are the targets of opportunity for the Global2000 shelter. I have listed the Strengths and Weaknesses of both competitors below.

ABC Corp. Strengths:

- ABC Corp. has been around since 1982, starting out as small manufacturer of concrete buildings for microwave communications.

- Their shelters can be found in all 50 states.

- They have the installation experience for installing telecom equipment, and have been doing so since 1991 in their manufacturing facility.

- They are the leading manufacturer of concrete structures for the telecom, education, and corrections markets.

- ABC Corp. shelters have a 10-year warranty.

- Concrete shelters provide better protection against equipment theft than do metal cabinets.
- Built more than 32,000 telecom shelters since 1982.
- They have the largest plant capacity in the industry because of their advanced European concrete processing equipment.
- Their shelter exteriors can be made to match existing structures.

ABC Corp. Weaknesses:
- Heavy, concrete shelters weigh anywhere from 20,000 to 40,000 pounds without telecom equipment installed.
- Serviceability for electrical panels and air conditioning must be completed outside in the elements.
- Typical footprint of shelter is 8'feet x 16' feet (128 Sq Ft), with an Effective size of 264.5 Sq Ft, due to the 42"inch buffer required for external access on 3 sides of the shelter.
- Storage, handling, and transport of units are difficult because of size and weight.
- Deployment of shelters is not as timely due to production lead times and transport.
- Support capabilities are limited to a single manufacturing site.

DEF Corp. Strengths:
- They have deployed over 10,000 building systems.
- DEF Corp. posted sales of $4.9 million last year. Their financial information was not broken out by product segment.
- DEF Corp. is also diverse in its product offerings; they offer modular buildings for education, utility control buildings, security structures, and pre-cast concrete fencing.
- They market themselves by stating; "Our team of experienced professionals is committed to doing whatever it takes to provide our customers with superior products and innovative solutions. We truly believe in quality and service and look forward to demonstrating this to you."
- DEF Corp. also offers electrical and mechanical installation at the factory.
- DEF Corp. also advertises low maintenance and a 50+ year life cycle structure.

DEF Corp. Weaknesses:
- They offer heavy concrete shelters weighing anywhere from 20,000 to 40,000 pounds without equipment installed.
- The company is small, having acquired the intellectual assets of Rohn Industries, who was previously a supplier to the telecom industry.
- DEF Corp. does not have the depth or expertise in this industry that either ABC Corp. or ASFCN has.
- Storage, handling, and transportation of these units are difficult because of size and weight.
- Support capabilities are limited to a single manufacturing site.

Comparison of competition

ABC Corp. is the leader in concrete shelters having been around since 1982. ABC Corp. posted sales of $37.5 million last year. Their financial information was not broken out by product segment however. ABC Corp. is diverse in their product offerings. They also provide precast concrete buildings for both schools and correctional facilities. ABC Corp. states that their units have a 10 year structural and roof warranty. They advertise themselves as the leader in equipment protection. They offer installation of customer telecom equipment at their manufacturing site. Additionally, they say that their units offer lower operating temperatures, thereby reducing high temperature shutdowns and battery damage that could result in voiding the warranty. They also advertise that concrete shelters offer better protection against network theft and vandalism.

DEF Corp. appears to be a distant second to ABC Corp. with sales of approximately $4.9 million for last year. This figure is 13% of ABC Corp.'s revenue for last year. DEF Corp. is also diverse in its product offerings. They also provide precast concrete, heavy gauge steel, steel frame, steel container, and light weight panelized building systems. They advertise themselves as a full service prefabricated concrete building manufacturer, specializing in pre-installed components and custom structures. They indicate that their building sizes are some of the largest in the industry; 64 to 10,000 Square Feet.

Comparison of Global2000

In contrast, Global2000 is the lightest, most compact shelter at a competitive cost. Global2000 has a multi-staged indoor mounted air conditioner eliminating the need for exterior access of servicing. The indoor unit also reduces the effective size of the unit because outside access is not needed. Global2000 has a secured and protected vestibule permitting interior access to the Air Conditioner and Electrical Service.

At the same time, the telecom equipment is secured in an environmentally controlled space. The concrete shelters do not have this option. Global2000 requires less site square footage than a concrete shelter. For example, when comparing both unit shelters, 8' foot by 16' feet, the concrete shelter requires a total of 264.5 Square Feet, whereas the Global2000 requires 156 Square Feet. This is a 41% reduction in the effective size of the unit. Global2000 requires access just from the front. The other 3 sides of the unit can be butted up against existing structures. The concrete shelter requires access from 3 sides. This restriction is due to a 42" inch buffer requirement from the surface of the unit for serviceability of the air conditioners or service panels. Bottom line, less square footage means lower site costs, saving your customer money every month.

Expected Industry Response

I would expect a strong response from both DEF Corp. and ABC Corp.. Initially, I could see both competitors come out and remind customers of the advantages of concrete shelters and their history. The heavy weight shelter business accounts for 60% of the current market. Our product presents a real threat to their livelihood, and I could visualize a very aggressive campaign on their part. Their response would most likely be to try and undermine our product by telling customers that concrete is stronger and that their product could stand up to the elements better than the Global2000 Shelter. They would also remind wireless customers that our product is new and that it has no history. In the long run however, I would expect that they would both see the Global2000 shelter as a real threat to their business. ABC Corp. and DEF Corp. will probably both come out with their own lightweight versions eventually.

After all, Global2000 is less than half the weight (4,000 to 6,500 pounds) of a concrete shelter (20,000 to 40,000 pounds). Global2000 provides weather protection for both personnel and equipment. I would remind both competitors that ASFCN has a global presence as well as a strong, top-tier customer relationships. In addition, we have a reputation for quality, with excellence in both engineering and manufacturing.

Financial Analysis

Based on the current make-up of the shelter market, cell sites consist of 60% heavy weight shelters (concrete), 30% light-weight shelters, and 10% cabinets. Based on the Wireless Association's historical data, new construction of cell sites is expected to be approximately 17, 175 new cell sites per year. We will be going after both the heavy weight and light-weight shelter market representing 15,458 cell sites per year. We expect to capture 10% per year for the first three years. In short, that represents 1718 shelters the first year, 3435 shelters the second year, and 5153 shelters the third year.

Below, I have listed monthly costs associated with an assembly operation to include fixed costs, variable costs, and a Break-even analysis. Fixed costs consist of a building lease for a 50,000 Square Feet at $3.00/ Square Foot.

Fixed Costs:		Employees:	
Facility – Lease -	$ 16,666.67	General Manager -	$7K/month
Utilities -	$ 5,000.00	Warehouse Manager -	$4.16K/month
Insurance -	$ 9,000.00	Quality Engineer -	$5K/month
Labor – Hourly -	$320,000.00	Manufacturing Engineer -	$5K/month

Labor – Salary - $ 30,280.00   Warehouse technicians x 3 - $4.8K/month
                       $380,946.67   Customer Service - $1.9K/month
                                          Facilities Technician - $2.4K/month

Direct Costs: **$30,280.00**

Material - $ 15,400.00
MOH @ 10% $ 1,540.00   Hourly Technicians (80) $25.00/hour
Labor- 64 hrs/unit $ 1,600.00   **$320,000.00**
                      $ 18,540.00

Sales Price: **$ 28,000.00/unit**

Contribution Margin:
CM = $28,000 - $18,540 = $9460.00

Break-even Analysis:
BE = $380,946.67 / $9460.00 = 40.27 Shelters

Product Pricing Structure

The shelter pricing reflected, provides for a 34% gross margin, which was typical of telecom pricing. We normally saw pricing anywhere from 30% to 40% gross margin in the telecom business. I went ahead and determined a price using the mark-up pricing formula. I decided to go with a 34% mark-up on these wireless shelters. I have listed my numbers below.

   Fixed Costs: $380,946.67
   Direct (Variable) Costs: $18,540.00

   Expected Unit Sales: 1718 first year

Unit Cost = $18,540.00 + $380,946.67/1718 = $18,540.00 + 222 = $18,762.00

Mark-up = $18,762.00/ (1 - .34) = $18,762/.66 = $28,427.27 ea.

Channels of Distribution

Our channels of distribution are controlled by our own resources. Our process is to identify a central staging area in each our markets that allows for delivery and storage of our cabinets. This storage facility is handled by the ASFCN Telecom Group. Both new and old cabinets as well as our new Global2000 shelters can be dispositioned at any of the central staging areas that we have. These central staging areas allow for us to control these units which may or may not have expensive radio gear installed in them. We also provide asset tracking of all units through a RFID program.

For Global2000, we will be using a push strategy for our marketing process. We have our own internal sales team dedicated to the wireless telecom group. We have a very strong relationship with our sales team and work with them hand in hand on developing customer solutions. Our sales team spends quite a bit of time at the factory talking with engineers as well as management to learn about the production process as well as items that the manufacturing group has come up with to improve production. The sales team is proficient in the language of the manufacturing group, so that when it comes time to understand customer needs or new configurations, they are able to talk with the customer as if they were one of the manufacturing engineers.

Integrated Marketing Communication

I plan on using opportunities with the media, conducting a Press Release, as well as introducing Global2000 at the next Supercomm show in Chicago, Illinois on October 26-28, 2010. Below, I have listed the means by which I hope to use Integrated Marketing Plan to introduce Mellennium, followed by a sample PR release.

Global2000 is targeted towards the communications industry, and offers customizable shelter that is cost-effective and light-weight, while offering the capabilities to house the latest technologies. We have the opportunity to raise the visibility of ASFCN Manufacturing Inc. through the Global2000 announcement, and remind customers of our company's full-service capabilities, which include build, installation, test, delivery, site installation, and commissioning of new sites and shelters.

Objectives
- Raise visibility and credibility for the ASFCN Manufacturing Inc. services
- Gain visibility for the Global2000 product to push sales

Strategies
- Secure press and analyst appointments
- Leverage the SuperComm show for additional visibility
- Utilize previous wins and partnerships as appropriate

Tactics

Press and Analyst Meetings

We plan on launching the Mellennium shelter two weeks prior to Supercomm and showcasing Global2000 at the event. This should create a better forum for coverage at Supercomm. We need to make sure that the product is available for customer purchase by this date. Assuming the product is ready early this year, we might be able to do some phone interviews with key analysts this spring, and possible do some phone interviews with the press shortly thereafter.

Supercomm

Some of the considerations for the SuperComm show will be putting together items as I have listed below for our PR needs.

- **Press release**: We need to have copies of a product fact sheet
- **Press kits**: Corporate Marketing will develop 25 press kits to mail in advance to the press and analysts who schedule phone conferences
- **Spokesperson**: Marketing or Sales will need to provide a spokesperson to conduct the interviews the week during the SuperComm show.

PRESS RELEASE

ASFCN MANUFACTURING LAUNCHES CUTTING EDGE COMMUNICATIONS SHELTER PLATFORM SOLUTION—GLOBAL2000

New York, NY, August 1, 2010, ASFCN Manufacturing, a business unit of ASFCN Technology Inc., today announced that it is offering a cutting edge communications shelter solution, Global2000. ASFCN Manufacturing developed Global2000 in response to enormous market demand for a shelter platform that achieves optimal balance between size, weight, functionality, and cost. Global2000's unique design and incorporation of state-of-the-art technologies will revolutionize the wireless communications shelter industries.

Specifically, Global2000 is a communications shelter solution that utilizes a panelized wall system, separate service and communications vestibules, internal air conditioning and electrical service, and innovative structural design and use of materials. This combination delivers the most space efficient, cost effective, easy to deploy and maintain, lightweight, and versatile shelter available to the marketplace. For example, the unique design of Global2000 requires 25% to 40% less site space than competing solutions and enables deployment in both ground level and rooftop settings. Global2000's open design supports all technologies utilized for wireless networks and can be easily adapted to individual customer demands.

ASFCN Manufacturing will unveil Global2000 at its booth at Supercomm 2010 in Chicago, Illinois on October 26th through 28th.

IMC Budget

For the Integrated Market Communications budget, we expect to provide a press release a couple of weeks prior to the Supercomm show in Chicago. We will unveil the Global2000 shelter at Supercomm. As part of our B2B strategy, we will be dedicating a sales team consisting of a Director of Sales, District Manager, and a couple of Sales Representatives to introduce and sell the Global2000 unit. Below, I have listed sales salaries, benefits, and their anticipated expenses.

Sales Team	Salary	Benefits		Total
Director of Sales	$110,000.	$38,500.		$148,500.
District Manager	$85,000.	$29,750.		$114,750.
Sales Representative x 2	$55,000.	$19,250.		$148,500.
				$411,750.00
Travel Expenses				$250,000.

Marketing Materials			
Global2000 Brochures – Artwork & Design			$10,000.
Global2000 Brochures – 750 folders			$1,000.
Global2000 Coffee Mugs – 500 Mugs			$1,750.
Global2000 Wireless Antenna Pens – 2500			$2,500.

Global2000 PR Campaign			$10,000.
Supercomm Entry Fee/Booth			$25,000.
	Grand Total		**$712,000.00**

Conclusion

The proposed product, Global2000, highlights our desire to enter the next-generation shelter product market. This project requires an initial fixed cost investment of $380K. The expected contribution margin per unit is $9.5K with a break-even point at about 40 shelters. The operational risks are low due to growing market demand and lack of significant competitive offerings. The sales and marketing expenses are expected to total $712K for the launch with the majority of spending on headcount allocation and Supercomm participation.

High Technology Manufacturing (Supermarket)

Highlights of this Marketing Plan:
1. Detailed target market discussion
2. Comprehensive competitive analysis
3. Good financials with NPV analysis

Executive Summary

The ASFCN ShopAssist is a product created to revolutionize the experience for grocery shoppers in targeted chains. The product is designed to engage technically savvy consumers and increase store loyalty. The goal of this marketing plan is to demonstrate the distinctiveness of the product and how its effective implementation and utilization can lead to higher revenues and higher customer retention for participating stores.

Our mission statement is straightforward: The ASFCN ShopAssist seeks to set the standard for superior store and customer interfacing, utilizing the latest smart-phone technology to distinguish member stores and enhance the overall experience for customers in new and dynamic ways.

Our goal in providing this product is to help bring the grocery shopping experience into the 21st century. The emergence of smart-phone technology and digital tracking capabilities has presented us an opportunity to help shoppers get more out of their trips to the store. We seek to engage the customer in ways that improve efficiency, help save them money on purchases, and create an attractive atmosphere that will solidify their loyalty to a participating store or chain. We have created the ASFCN ShopAssist through an intuitive process that mirrors the normal tendencies of a wide span of shoppers. This will result in immediate recognition of its relevance by customers as they experience the personalized nature of the product to their own shopping history and patterns.

We have examined potential competitors and have identified two that are currently not actively engaged in our markets nor utilizing the same type of technology. We believe our novel approach and targeting untapped markets will negate any effect in the short and mid-term range. Our target market is the NorthWest region and is tracked at the zip-code level.

We are pricing this on a fixed percentage revenue model with a contracted 8% of all store revenues generated by ASFCN ShopAssist users. This will allow us to realize a positive net result as of the end of the second year. We forecast year over year growth for each of the first five years with a five-year realized profit of more than $780,000. Our marketing and promotional efforts will be in conjunction with each chain's marketing strategy, and the costs of promotion will be shifted from us to participating chains as the initial launch phase is concluded.

The marketplace is ready for the technology that the ASFCN ShopAssist offers. Consumers are become more technically savvy every year. The ASFCN ShopAssist fits with the middle to upper-middle class target market that we have identified. We anticipate that the success of this initial endeavor will create new opportunities that are customer generated and allow for significant growth and penetration into multiple markets throughout the country.

SWOT Analysis

Strengths
- First to market in the United States and Canada
- Customer specificity and customization.
- Ability to be used in any participating store throughout the country.
- Proprietary software already designed and ready for rapid implementation.
- IT personnel within each grocery chain can modify the software for enhanced customer personalization.

Weaknesses
- Uncertainty of level of engagement by consumers and grocery chain leadership.
- Lack of commitment by any major regional chains.
- Relies on those customers with smart-phones.
- Low visibility as a start-up company with no existing brand awareness.

Opportunities
- New technology offers a marketing advantage to early adopter chains in any given region.
- Successful implementation of the program can result in increased customer loyalty.
- Early success will build the case for swift and broad expansion to other regions of the country.
- Chance to highlight the ASFCN ShopAssist at the National Grocers Association annual conference.

Threats
- Fluctuating costs of hardware supply (key fob devices and the need for replacements for lost devices).
- Increased production and commercialization of the Smart Shopping Cart initiative by ABC Corp. or other competitor.
- The risk that technology like the ASFCN ShopAssist will be viewed as too technical and complex for the average shopper.

Target Market
The target market for the ASFCN ShopAssist is regional supermarket chains with an established

digital infrastructure to support the required software. It is primarily a business-oriented market with participating stores directly marketing to their consumers and communities. The consumer is a secondary target, as ASFCN ShopAssist will require broad customer engagement to be successful.

Segmentation

Geographic
- We will begin in the northwest region and focus on two identified chains: Quality Markets, Incorporated and American Food Depot.
- The initial targeted population is 150,000.

Demographic
- Participating stores will be in zip codes with median annual incomes greater than $60,000. To date, this includes 8 zip codes and approximately 145,000 people serviced by a total of 12 pilot stores.
- This will primarily focus on families with parents holding college degrees and a majority of homes having one working parent and a significant percentage (33%) of families with two working parents in professional fields.

Psychographic
- ASFCN ShopAssist will appeal to Innovators and Achievers alike.
- Its reliance on smart-phone technology and its novel approach to the shopping experience will engage discriminating consumers who want to be utilizing the most advanced tools available to enhance their regular activities such as grocery shopping.

The rationale for the chosen markets is familiarity and access. Both Quality Markets and American Food Depot have a reputation for being cutting edge in their approaches to customer engagement. They are not main competitors for one another, being owned by the same international conglomerate: International Food Products. Quality Markets offers a higher end gourmet experience while American Food Depot provides a more conventional grocery set-up. The vice president of consumer marketing oversees the marketing directors of both chains and is intent on incorporating technology into the shopping experience in both settings. This provides a favorable market climate for the ASFCN ShopAssist.

The selected market has the potential for significant growth and early adoption of a product like the ASFCN ShopAssist. Segmenting within the specific geodemographic parameters listed above fits well with the psychographic segment that we are trying to reach. The zip code data that we are intent on utilizing is also the data already used by both selected chains to market to their respective customer bases.

The breakdown of the market is as follows:

- **Who**: Residents of eight specific zip codes in the NorthWest states with a median yearly income of $60,000 and who currently utilize smart-phone technology.

- **How Measured**: We will utilize the existing demographic data maintained by each chain's corporate quality improvement departments. As well, the initial application process for each participating consumer will include specific demographic criteria that will help shape further rollout efforts of the product.

- **How Sustained**: We will work with each chains' marketing department to craft unique messages geared to their particular customer base. There will be initial marketing surges at each store and in the local media in the first month of the pilot period. As well, the IT department for both chains will be fully trained and prepared to handle all technological difficulties that may arise initially.

- **Accessibility**: The ASFCN ShopAssist is designed for anyone with a current smart-phone. The software is compatible with multiple digital platforms. The app download will take on average one to two minutes to fully download. The key fob will be immediately activated once a customer signs on for the device. Each store will be able to test and confirm the proper functioning of a key fob before the customer leaves the store.

- **Ability to Reach Targeted Market**: We identified two chains with the precise demographics we believe will respond best to the ASFCN ShopAssist. The ability to reach this market is accounted for in our selection of the two chains. There will be collaborative efforts with the marketing directors at each chain. We are aiming to reach both current customers and consumers not loyal to any particular store in the given zip codes that fit in with our demographic targeting strategy.

These market factors will continuously be monitored and evaluated. The flexibility of the ASFCN ShopAssist will allow individual stores to customize their programs to further engage their particular target base. After six months, we are confident that the impact of the ASFCN ShopAssist will be accurately assessed. Its success will be measured and utilized to justify expansion in later years into additional targeted markets throughout the country.

Competitive Analysis

Grocers in every community are increasingly facing stiffer competition as they struggle to maintain customer loyalty. To date, there is no widespread competition in the market for the ASFCN ShopAssist. That could change in the near future as a handful of companies either have limited market penetration or are researching different technological platforms for the food market in particular. We will examine two of these potential competitors here to help give context to the market in the near future.

The first product is the Shopping Helper, designed by ABC Corp. and limited to use in select towns in New York State since 2004-2005. As described in a recent articlesbase.com article, "The Shopping Helper is a small tablet that you activate with your CDE Supermarket card" (2010). It goes on to explain that the product is used to register personal coupons and aisle history based on the customer's card information.

Analysis of Shopping Helper

Strengths

- Each participating store has Helper devices on site and available for use by customers.
- Each device comes with a detached wand for item barcode scanning.
- The device will highlight items on sale based on the customer's shopping history.
- The Shopping Helper keeps a running cost tally of items scanned by the wand.
- It offers the ability to enter an item and receive its exact location in the store.

Weaknesses

- The cost of set-up and implementation for the average store is estimated at $160,000 (Senne, 2005).
- There is an inherent risk of damage from normal wear and tear, the device being dropped, liquid spills, and system battery failure.
- Every customer must take time to log in at a store computer each visit to activate the system and obtain a device.
- It must be carried for those wanting to use a basket rather than a cart, thus increasing the chance of damage and annoying the customer now required to handle a bulky device in addition to his or her groceries.
- There are a finite number of devices allocated per store.

CDE Supermarket partnered with ABC CORP. in 2003 to begin to formulate a plan to bring these devices to market. The devices were tested in 2004 and rolled out in select New York locations in 2005. The current version of the device is called Barcode Me!; it is being used in select stores throughout the northeast. Its market penetration is still somewhat limited. CDE Supermarket has 377 stores in the northeast, but its website reveals that only 200 of them have this technology. This equates to about 53% of all of their sites.

Their target market appears to include a large demographic. Participating stores are located in both urban and suburban settings. Barcode Me! is part of a larger initiative in the stores to be more customer-centric. In addition, these stores highlight the availability for self-checkout and family friendly lanes, to name a few. By casting a wide market net, they will possibly overlap with the ASFCN ShopAssist's targeted market in parts of Los Angeles. To date, CDE Supermarket has modest penetration in the areas where the ASFCN ShopAssist is going to be rolled out initially.

Assuming that the Barcode Me! device could further expand into our targeted market, we think it is important to highlight the distinct advantages of the ASFCN ShopAssist that will distinguish it from Barcode Me! from the start:

- The cost per store of implemeting the ASFCN ShopAssist system will be significantly less.

- The hardware consists of a key fob that is very durable and easily replaced as well as a phone app that will be downloaded for free by customers.

- There is no need for customers to log in at the store after they are initially activated in the system. Once activated, they will be able to use the product at every participating store within both chains.

- There is no limit (based on number of equipped carts) to the number of customers who can participate.

All of these reasons reinforce the convenience for the customer and the consumer perception of customer-centric stores for the chains. The software is intuitive and readily mastered by anyone with general exposure to smart-phone technology and the use of apps. We do not anticipate a significant response from CDE Supermarket once we launch the ASFCN ShopAssist. They are currently not heavily present in our targeted market. Where they are present, we expect them to increase their marketing of the total shopping experience rather than just focusing on their Barcode Me! technology. Our response to this will be to continue to market with a consistent message to our specific consumer pool. We will focus specifically on our distinctives listed above and use them to increase our market presence.

The second potential competitor we will examine is the Grocery Maid marketed by DEF Technology Inc., Inc. The device is an interactive touchscreen tablet mounted on the handle of a shopping cart. According to the company's website, it utilizes wireless technology and offers a variety of customer tools to enhance the shopping experience.

Analysis for the Grocery Maid:

Strengths
- Mounted on the handle of each cart and activated by movement.
- Includes a barcode scanner that allows it to scan items and speed up the checkout process.
- It highlights items on sale and new product launches.

- Customers who create shopping lists on the store site from home have access to their lists on the interactive screen once they swipe their store card.

- Technology allows customer shopping patterns to be captured for future customized marketing.

Weaknesses
- The cost of set-up and implementation varies but is believed to be around $500 per console (Senne, 2005).

- Devices are limited by the number of carts available.

- Shoppers must use an equipped cart even when all they need is a basket to do their shopping.

- Replacement of damaged consoles can be costly and time consuming.

- Possible threat of system failure resulting in lost information and time.

The Grocery Maid device has been available in its current form since 2007. The Canadian based company has received favorable reviews in the media and is looking to penetrate markets througout the U.S. and Canada. To date, there has been uptake in some Canadian metropolitan areas and in several Food King locations in the southeast region. It has received favorable reviews by industry groups both in Canada and the U.S.

We believe that DEF Technology Inc. is looking to expand into multiple regions of the country. Their website indicates that they are targeting anyone who wants to have an efficient, successful shopping experience. This obviously will envelop our current target segment. However, their regional presence is not an immediate threat to a successful launch of the ASFCN ShopAssist in our identified geography.

As with the Barcode Me! device, we can envision a future expansion into our markets by the Grocery Maid system. We believe that the following specific advantages will help differentiate us from the Grocery Maid in effective ways:

- The cost per store of implementing the ASFCN ShopAssist system will be significantly less (projected to be a percentage fee for all revenues tied to the use of the ShopAssist product in participating stores).

- The hardware consists of a key fob that is very durable and easily replaced as well as a phone app that will be downloaded for free by customers.

- There is no limit (based on number of equipped carts) to the number of customers who can participate at any given time.

- Quick purchases not requiring a cart will be easily handled by the ASFCN ShopAssist.

This, again, comes down to convenience for the customer and data for the grocery chains. It will help improve efficiencies, tailor sales to specific customers, and enhance the overall shopping experience for customers. This, in turn, will solidifiy consumer loyalty and increase word-of-mouth advertising within the community. This will prepare our client stores well for when the Grocery Maid system appears in our geographic areas. We will highlight our distinct advantages and focus on customer-specific marketing for each of our sites.

Financial Analysis

In this section, we will address the forecast for the ASFCN ShopAssist. We will present a break-even analysis and a net present value analysis. We will begin with the break-even analysis.

Break-even Analysis:

Fixed Costs (monthly):

Supplied Equipment:	$24000
Payroll:	$10500
Communications:	$3000
Business Operations:	$2500

Variable Costs (monthly):

Service Calls:	20%
Replacement of Damaged Equipment:	12%
Smart-phone Application Updates:	5%

System Cost Per Chain: 8% of revenues derived from use of the ASFCN ShopAssist

Assumptions:

Initial Monthly Revenue per Store:	$2000
Number of Participating Stores per Chain:	12
Total Revenue per Chain per Month:	$24000
Total Revenue for both Chains per Month:	$48000
Monthly Fixed Costs:	$40000

$CM =$ Selling Price − Direct (Variable) Costs
48000 - 17760
$CM =$ 30240

$BE =$ Fixed Costs/CM

$BE =$ 40000/30240

$BE =$ 1.3227513

The required monthly amount to break even across the stores in both chains is $2645.50 per store. This is an increase in single store revenue of $645.50 per month (@32% increase in revenue).

Net Present Value (NPV) Analysis:

NPV Calculation at standard 8% discount rate of return:

Year	Net Cash Flow	PVIF @ 8%	Present Value
One	-$8256	0.9259	-$7644
Two	$180444	0.8573	$154695
Three	$312528	0.7938	$248085
Four	$431376	0.7350	$317061
Five	$567,996	0.6806	$386578

NPV = $398,775

The initial cost of the project to outfit each chain is $350,000 for a total cost of $700,000. With the anticipated growth in initial stores, we believe that the ASFCN ShopAssist will actually prove to have a positive return on investment after year four (1.7%). After year five, the return on investment is forecasted to be 52.8% for all stores combined in the two original participating chains.

Year 1: forecasted growth of 30% over initial monthly per store revenue ($2000)

$2,600 * 24 stores = $62,400 - $23,088 (direct costs)
= $39,312
$39,312 (revenue) - $40,000 (fixed costs) = -$688/month
= -$8,256 annual loss

Year 2: forecasted growth of 40% over previous year

$3,640 * 24 stores = $87,360 - $32,323 (direct costs)
= $55,037
$55,037 (revenue) - $40,000 (fixed costs) = $15,037/month
=$180,444 annual profit

Year 3: forecasted growth of 20% over previous year

$4,368 * 24 stores = $104,832 - $38,788 (fixed costs)
= $66,044
$66,044(revenue) - $40,000 (direct costs) = $26,044/month
= $312,528 annual profit

Year 4: forecasted growth of 15% over previous year

$5,023 * 24 stores = $120,552 - $44,604 (fixed costs)
= $75,948
$75,948(revenue) - $40,000 (direct costs) = $35,948/month
=$431,376 annual profit

Year 5: forecasted growth of 15% over previous year

$5,776 * 24 stores = $138,624 - $51,291 (fixed costs)
= $87,333
$87,333(revenue) - $40,000 (direct costs) = $47,333/month
= $567,996 annual profit

Five year realized profit: $784,088 (52.8%)

Sensitivity Analysis: We will briefly look at an analysis of market conditions where the variable is the rate of growth over our initial period of time. We will consider the results utilizing the 8% rate of return and the present value interest factor (PVIF).

Sub-optimal Scenario:
Flat rate of utilization after initial launch and no incremental uptake or growth over the first five years.

Initial 30% growth leads to an annual loss of -$8256 in the first year. Subsequent flat years with no growth will result in a net present value of -$33,575 and will prevent a successful introduction of the ASFCN ShopAssist system into the market as currently configured.

Normal Scenario:
Rate of growth will be in line with our above-mentioned forecasts. We believe our growth rates over the initial five year period will allow us to realize a positive return after year four and substantial return on investment at year five.

Good Scenario:
Rate of percentage growth will outpace our current forecast year over year. This will result in an accelerated timeline in terms of profitability. This could also be realized by having a lower discounted rate of return than the 8% we are using in our current planning.

Pricing Structure
We have examined numerous factors in setting the price for the ASFCN ShopAssist. We accounted for expected fixed and variable costs as broken down in the break-even analysis.

Our pricing objective falls under the product-quality leadership category. We intend to raise the perception of our participating chains by helping set them apart from their competitor through the utilization of the ASFCN ShopAssist.

We believe there is a need for strategic target costing. The initial cost to us for implementation is significant. At $350,000 per chain, we are aware of the need to plan for both recoupment of investment and realization of long-term growth. Our pricing is based directly on the revenues generated by in-store use of our technology. We believe that the partnering aspect of our contracts with the chains is fairly represented in the 8% share of revenues we will receive. As the use of the ASFCN ShopAssist increases, our revenues will track on the same trajectory.

Our year one gross revenues are forcasted to be $471,744 with an expected annual loss of $8,256 in that first year. By year three, we expect our annual gross revenue to be $792,258 with a profit of $312,528. Our set pricing will allow us to move past break-even during year four, provided that our growth projections are met consistently in the first four years.

We are fully aware that the emergence of a competitor into our regions in competing grocery chains is a possibility. This will be a factor to consider once it is in place and may require revised forecasting going forward to account for it. At this time, we believe our selected markets are primed to experience exclusive exposure to the ASFCN ShopAssist technology without any immediate known threats on the near-term horizon.

As we analyze the pricing of our two closest competitors (Grocery Maid and Shopping Helper), we feel our pricing is set in such a way as to encourage sustained growth. According to available data, we understand the cost per store to implement the Shopping Helper to be $160,000 charged to the customer. As well, the Grocery Maid device is thought to be around $500 per console (Senne, 2005). With our stable 8% revenue share, we believe that our customers will feel more at ease knowing that we will be compensated on an ongoing basis and only with revenues actually generated by use of our technology. The stiff up-front cost of implementation of the Shopping Helper or the need to purchase large quantities of Grocery Maid devices could likely be prohibitive for either system to rapidly or broadly expand into our targeted markets.

Given the limited scope of the initial project (2 chains comprised of 24 stores in specific regions within 2 bordering states), we will be acting as direct providers to our customers. We will discuss channel distribution issues in the next section.

Channels of Distribution

Our Sales group will deal with the single vice president of consumer marketing and two marketing directors. The group is comprised of a group leader, two technology liaisons (one for each chain), and an administrative assistant. Our technology liaisons will be in constant contact with their respective marketing directors and store managers. They will serve as direct channel service providers. These liaisons will have access to the escalated support group located at company headquarters as needed. The administrative assistant will handle all non-technical issues and track and compile usage data for reporting back to the company's executive committee. The group leader will insure that the systems are operational and that joint marketing efforts for increased use of the ASFCN ShopAssist are optimized.

We believe that we can reduce additional costs, at least in the initial stages, by keeping all operations internal to the company. Projected growth, if realized, will require the effective development and implementation of a distribution channel strategy. Our forecast for this is in the 5-10 year range currently. We will reassess all operations on an annual basis and run projection models to identify the right timing of a move to channel distribution.

Our production of key fobs is being supervised by our operations department. They will manage stocked quantities for both growing demand within stores and replacements of faulty or damaged fobs. Our company information technology department will manage and service the actual program software as well as identify and configure all smart-phone application updates on an ongoing basis.

We envision a push promotional effort, working in concert with store management and marketing within both chains. Our success hinges on utilization growth. The chains' advertising efforts will need to be geared towards awareness and knowledge. Their customers need to understand how the availability of the ASFCN ShopAssist will significantly improve their overall shopping experience and help them save time and money. As awareness and familiarity grows for customers initially exposed to it and having a positive experience, we expect that word-of-mouth marketing will help build local momentum.

Each store is going to participate in a coordinated launch of the ASFCN ShopAssist once it is rolled out. Our "Guru Group" will be part of the planning team to help prepare for a successful introduction. Early adopters will be rewarded with additional significant savings as well as earn multiple entries into drawings for a free trip to the Caribbean (one to be offered at each store). Each store will also have a contracted IT person available during the launch (along with their own fully trained ASFCN ShopAssist specialist) to make the sign-up process happen with minimal glitches. The goal is to appeal to each customers' desire to have a first-rate experience every time they shop.

Integrated Marketing Communication and Budget

Our advertising is going to work in tandem with the participating chains' efforts to leverage the appeal of the ASFCN ShopAssist in their communities. The marketing directors of each chain are responsible for the development and implementation of a plan geared specifically towards our product. The "Guru Group" will assist in the marketing efforts. Initial publicity will consist of a number of activities, utilizing print media, radio ad time, direct mailings to targeted consumers, links on the chains' specific websites, and visibility on particular social media outlets.

The primary objective is to distinguish the ASFCN ShopAssist as a unique tool that will increase traffic into participating stores and strengthen loyalty of current customers. Both stores already track customer flow and volume on a daily, weekly, and monthly basis. We will measure changes in the volume for the first three months after our product is launched. We will tie this to the number of sign-ups for the ASFCN ShopAssist for each store. The software in our system is able to tally the purchases for each customer using the ASFCN ShopAssist. This will allow us to gauge the level of penetration of the product on a monthly basis.

The launch of the ASFCN ShopAssist is crucial to establishing momentum and buzz from the start. We are preparing to create front-page advertisements for all participating stores' weekly circular for the entire first month. The cost of this will be absorbed by the chains marketing budget. In addition, we will a day of free seminars at each store over the first month to engage early adopters and keep technical glitches to a minimum. Grocery giveaways and other in-store promotional activities will accompany the introduction of the product.

We will provide advertising support for the first 3 months in two specific areas: radio spots and newspaper advertisements in Sunday editions. The radio spots will be 30 seconds in length and will focus on the primary news station heard throughout NorthWest region: KIIS station. The average rate for a 30 second spot on this station is $383. If we air the ad 10 times per day, the rate goes down by 20% per airing. This would be $306.40 per airing or $3,064 per day. This volume will allow us to select the desired time slots we are targeting for maximum exposure. We have identified 6:30am-8:30am, 12:00pm-1:00pm, and 4:30pm-6:30pm as the time periods in which we will have our ad aired twice per hour. Our plan is to run the radio spots on Mondays, Wednesdays, and Fridays for the first 3 months. The projected cost for this period of time is $110,304. After this initial period, the chains will assume ongoing advertising costs through their own marketing departments.

The primary regional newspaper that we are targeting is the Los Angeles Daily newspaper. Its coverage extends well into Los Angeles and serves the entire targeted area for us. Our part of the print advertising plan is again in the initial 3 months. We will run half page ads (one for each chain separately) in the Sunday editions. This will equate to a total of 12 Sundays and a resulting 24 half page advertisements. According to research, this will cost $1,892 per advertisement per Sunday (philly.com, 2010). The total would be $45,408. As with the radio advertising, the chains will take over print marketing after the initial launch phase is complete.

Our promotional budget for the first year will be front-loaded in the initial 3 months. It entails our radio and print efforts as well as in-store promotional items. These promotional items (smart-phone protective cases, pens, t-shirts, and decorative keychains) will cost a total of $2,400. These three components will bring the promotional budget to $158,112. All other promotional costs are being assumed by our participating stores. The budget is initially accounted for in our implementation per chain cost (up to $80,000 of the $350,000) and will be recouped over the first 3 years based on our above-stated financial forecast. The long-term success of the ASFCN ShopAssist will allow us to adopt a recoupment and reinvestment cycle as we expand into more regions of the country.

Conclusion

Due to the growing interest of the grocery assistance device product category and the increase implementation of competitive products by major supermarket chains, ASFCN decides to enter the market with its ASFCN ShopAssist product. We believe that our product has superior features and can successfully compete with existing offerings such as Shopping Helper and Grocery Maid. A 5-year NPV, based on a 8% discount rate, is determined to be $398,775.

Epilogue

In this book, I have presented you with the "ingredients" of a typical marketing plan and examples from various industries. As you can see, there's no single template of marketing plan that works for every product or service on this planet. If this is your first time to write a marketing plan for your organization, I highly suggest you to review a copy of marketing plan that has previously been presented to management. In this way, you can get a rough idea about the required document format so that you are not wasting time to invent the wheel. Remember, it is not a competition of writing the longest marketing plan on earth. As you have already discovered from the examples that I have shown in this book, no two pieces of marketing plan look 100% the same. So, never try to copy every section from the book or else you will be producing a 50-page document that your boss won't have time to read. In my opinion, a short-and-concise piece is all you need.

To those who are browsing this book right now at Chapters/Indigo, just pay for it and evaluate the book leisurely at home for 2 weeks. Don't stand in the aisle for the whole afternoon! Remember to keep your original receipt if you intend to get a full-refund at the bookstore later.

If you have purchased this book as part of Dr. Wong's course, thank you. I hope this little book can help you write better papers to earn higher grades. On the other hand, if you have just downloaded this book from those illegal web sites and intend to keep a copy in your computer for future reference, you have 3 options:

1. Go to iUniverse's official web site to purchase a legitimate electronic copy. I have intentionally made the ebook version affordable (about US$10) so that my students can enjoy it without breaking an arm and a leg. Helping you to understand the concept of intellectual properties is part of my teaching objectives.

2. Make a donation to your local charity or become a volunteer. I really mean it. If you absolutely don't want to pay the publisher for whatever reasons, please at least make a difference to help other people in your community.

3. Do nothing, if you think stealing is the right thing to do.

Have a great day and thanks for taking time to read my work.

Cheers,

Ken

References

Arens, W. F., Weigold, M. F., & Arens, C. (2008). Contemporary Advertising (12th ed.). New York: McGraw Hill Higher Education.

Armstrong, G., & Kotler, P. (2009). Principles of Marketing (13th ed.). Alexandria, VA: Prentice Hall.

Belch, G. E., & Belch, M. A. (2008). Advertising and Promotion: An Integrated Marketing Communications Perspective (8th ed.). New York: McGraw-Hill/Irwin.

Boyd, H., Mullins, J., & Walker, O. (2009). Marketing Management: A Strategic Decision-making Approach (7th ed.). New York: McGraw-Hill.

Cannon, J., Jr.., Mccarthy, E. J., & Perreault, W. (2008). Basic Marketing (17th ed.). New York: McGraw-Hill/Irwin.

Cateora, P. R., & Graham, J. (2006). International Marketing (McGraw Hill/Irwin Series in Marketing) (13th ed.). New York: McGraw-Hill/Irwin.

Cateora, P. R., Graham, J. L., & Papadopoulos, N. (2008). International Marketing (2nd Canadian ed.) Toronto: McGraw-Hill Ryerson.

Crane, F. G., Kerin, R. A., Hartley, S. W., Berkowitz, E. N. & Rudelius, W. (2006). Marketing. (6th Canadian Ed.). Toronto: McGraw-Hill Ryerson

Hill, C. W. (2010). International Business (8th ed.). New York: Mcgraw Hill Higher Education.

Kotler, P. & Keller, K. L. (2008). Marketing Management (13th Edition). Alexandria, VA: Prentice Hall.

Porter, M.E. (1979). How Competitive Forces Shape Strategy, *Harvard business Review*, March/April 1979.

Porter, M.E. (2008). The Five Competitive Forces That Shape Strategy, *Harvard business Review*, January 2008.

The Star, the Dog, the Cow and the Question Mark (2010) BCG History: 1968. Retrieved from http://www.bcg.com/about_bcg/history/history_1968.aspx

Index